MAKING TEACHING WORK

MAKING TEACHING WORK

'Teaching Smarter' in Post-Compulsory Education

Phil Race and Ruth Pickford

SAGE Publications
Los Angeles • London • New Delhi • Singapore

First published 2007

SAGE Publications Ltd
1 Oliver's Yard
55 City Road
London EC1Y 1SP

SAGE Publications Inc
2455 Teller Road
Thousand Oaks, California 91320

SAGE Publications India Pvt Ltd
B 1/I 1 Mohan Cooperative Industrial Area
Mathura Road, Post Bag 7,
New Delhi 110 044

SAGE Publications Asia-Pacific Pte Ltd
33 Pekin Street #02-01
Far East Square
Singapore 048763

British Library Cataloguing in Publication data

A catalogue record for this book is available from the British Library

ISBN 978-1-4129-3606-4
ISBN 978-1-4129-3607-1 (pbk)

Library of Congress Control Number: 2007922038

Typeset by Dorwyn, Wells, Somerset
Printed in Great Britain by The Cromwell Press, Trowbridge, Wilts
Printed on paper from sustainable resources

Contents

About this book

Most great teachers really *care* about their teaching, and *care* about their students' learning. However, even this is not always enough to guarantee that teaching will really work. In this book, we offer detailed suggestions on what you can *do* to ensure that your best intentions come to fruition. This isn't intended to be a book to be read from beginning to end, but rather a resource to be a companion to you at various stages in your teaching.

Chapter 1 'Why teach smarter?' is intended to remind you of (or alert you to) some of the changes affecting higher education nowadays, and to get you thinking about some of the targets to aspire to in terms of excellent teaching and learning.

Chapter 2 'Beyond learning cycles and styles' will, we hope, get you thinking about teaching and learning as processes which involve feelings and emotions on both sides, and which need us to maximise channels of communication between ourselves and our students.

Chapter 3 'Supporting individual learning and responding to learning needs' addresses the fact that the range of individual learning needs has never been greater in higher education than it is now. This chapter offers suggestions for responding to as many of these needs as you can in the design of your teaching.

Chapter 4 'Working with small groups' looks at a range of aspects of designing and running seminars and tutorials, and helping students to learn from and with each other.

Chapter 5 'Working with large groups' explores the high-profile contexts of lectures and whole-group teaching. We've included in this chapter numerous suggestions for handling large-group teaching, with the emphasis remaining on ensuring that students' learning happens effectively.

Chapter 6 'Dealing with disruptive students' picks up some of the threads of those things which can go wrong both in small- and large-group contexts, and offers suggestions for minimising the effect of some of the most common manifestations of disruption.

Chapter 7 'Developing online learning' explores the rapidly-developing area of digital learning and examines the issues relating to the use of modern information and communications technologies.

Chapter 8 'Managing assessment and feedback' looks at what we can do to ensure that the sharp end of students' learning experiences is addressed systematically and sympathetically. We also look at how to maximise the payoff from the time and energy we put into designing assessment, and giving feedback (and feed-ahead) to our students.

Chapter 9 on 'Differentiation' offers suggestions about how we can make teaching work simultaneously both for high-fliers and low-fliers in our classrooms and lecture theatres.

Chapter 10 on 'Addressing student satisfaction' looks at how we can go about making sure that not only is our teaching working well, but also that it is *felt* to be working well by our students, and *seen* to be working well in the feedback from students about their learning experience.

Chapter 11 on 'Finding your feet as a new or part-time member of staff' is included for the benefit of part-time staff and full-time staff new in post alike.

Chapter 12 on 'Putting your best foot forward' aims to ensure that your teaching work is *seen* to be working well when observed by colleagues, or others.

This book aims to help you to address the following key questions:

1. *What's changing* in post-compulsory education, and how do the changes affect your teaching? (Chapter 1)
2. How can you know whether your teaching is '*excellent*'? (Chapter 2)
3. How can you introduce *inclusive practice* and support special learning needs? (Chapter 3)
4. How can you respond to *individual learning needs* more efficiently and effectively? (Chapter 3)
5. How can you work with *small groups* in the classroom? (Chapter 4)
6. How can you effectively design *teamwork*? (Chapter 4)
7. How can you engage students in *large group learning*? (Chapter 5)
8. How can you *prevent and deal with disruptive student behaviour*? (Chapter 6)
9. What can *online learning* do? (Chapter 7)
10. How best can you utilise *assessment and feedback* to make teaching work with your students? (Chapter 8)
11. How can you design delivery and assessment to accurately *differentiate student performance*? (Chapter 9)
12. What can you do in your teaching to increase your *students' satisfaction* with their learning? (Chapter 10)
13. What particular needs have *part-time staff*, especially when starting a new appointment? (Chapter 11)

14 How best can you *show that you have planned* systematically and effectively to make your teaching work well? (Chapter 12)

We hope that you will find our book really useful, and will quickly find the parts which are most helpful in your own contexts. We wish you every success in making your teaching work well.

Acknowledgements

We are very grateful to countless colleagues and students upon whose experience we have built in writing this book. We are both particularly grateful to Sally Brown who has inspired and motivated us, and contributed essential thinking and ideas to several parts of the book. We are also thankful to Sheila Johnston and Heather Clothier for their support and encouragement.

Phil Race
Ruth Pickford
January 2007

1

Why teach smarter?

This chapter addresses the following questions:

- What's changing in post-compulsory education, and how do the changes affect your teaching?
- Why is it important to teach smarter to retain your students?

What is changing in post-compulsory education?

In Australia, China, New Zealand, Scandinavia and the Netherlands as well as in the UK there is an ongoing debate about the nature of post-compulsory education and how to guarantee good quality teaching. For example, the UK government's White Paper in 2003 stated that 'Institutions must properly *reward* their best teaching staff: all who teach must take their task seriously' (DfES, 2003: our emphasis). It also indicated that 'Student choice will increasingly work to drive up quality, supported by much better information'. This was the stimulus for the National Student Survey to which we refer in Chapters 8 and 10. A significant example of this new concentration on excellent teaching is the establishment by the Higher Education Funding Council for England (HEFCE) of 74 Centres of Excellence for Teaching and Learning in England.

In 2005 the granting of university titles in the UK became no longer conditional on research degree awarding powers, enabling colleges with excellent teaching to become universities in their own right. In 2007 the UK's Further Education colleges are also set to obtain their own degree awarding powers and market forces will mean that managers and teachers will need to be even smarter in their approaches to teaching if they are to recruit and retain students.

How does this translate into practice?

We are certainly witnessing a growing interest in delivery processes as well as curriculum content, with less focus on what is taught and more on how learning is fostered. There is huge potential to use technology to impact positively on curriculum delivery, assessment, evaluation and student feedback and discussion. Furthermore, there is a growing body of research into what constitutes effective learning and teaching, particularly linked to international initiatives on the scholarship of teaching. More and more institutions are establishing Centres for Research into Higher Education, all of which are aiming to gain a better understanding of what constitutes really good practice in learning and teaching. Almost all higher education institutions in the UK, and many international universities and colleges, now place great importance on training for teaching in post-compulsory education using an evidence-based, research-informed approach to teaching (see http://www.seda.ac.uk/).

Changing patterns of learning

Patterns of curriculum delivery are altering significantly in post-compulsory education. We are seeing extensive replacement of mass lectures with workshops and problem-based learning classes, while at the same time such lectures as remain tend to be larger and less personal. Individual tutorials are becoming rarer and seminar group sizes are increasing. At a time when it is recognised that students, particularly those from disadvantaged backgrounds, need individualised support to assure retention, financial restraints are making it harder and harder to offer this. Considerable efforts are being made to develop reusable learning objects which can be used cost-effectively in a variety of contexts, but with the potential danger of even greater depersonalisation of the learning experience of students.

Changes to the student body

The introduction of tuition fees has changed the way that education is viewed by many students and parents; there exists a more litigious culture in which students who feel they have not got value for money in terms of tuition are increasingly likely to sue institutions. Many institutions are also witnessing increasing numbers of students behaving strategically, asking not just 'How can I do well on this course?', but also more commonly now that most students are undertaking some part-time work 'What is the minimum I can do on this course to scrape a bare pass, since I don't have time to do more than that?'

Changes affecting staff

A changing context in post-compulsory education means that traditional roles are shifting and blurring, with academics, learning technologists, learning support staff and information retrieval specialists coming together to work in learning teams who can develop learning environments and materials. With a more structured approach to the management of curriculum design and delivery, there is often perceived to be less autonomy for individual teachers, which many see as the onset of higher levels of managerialism (see Braun and Merrien, 1999). There are now conflicting pressures on teachers to balance teaching, research, administration, community service and other duties, with a greater emphasis on accountability. In the UK, for example, the HEFCE's Transparent Approach to the Costing process (TRAC – see http://www.hefce.ac.uk/finance/fundinghe/TransparencyReview/) requires staff to keep records of the balance of the different kinds of duties in which they engage to enable a robust and accurate local costing of teaching and other activities. Employment practices are changing too with a tendency towards casualisation of the workforce, with the employment of more part-time staff, and the increased use of short-term contracts.

Changing assessment

Assessment too is changing, with an impetus towards student-centred assessment aligning with more student-centred approaches to teaching and hence a greater emphasis on group, peer- and self-assessment (see Chapter 8) with clients and other stakeholders being involved in assessment. We are also seeing more diverse methods and approaches used (such as portfolios, in-tray exercises, assessed seminars, posters, reflective accounts and critical incidents, annotated bibliographies and so on), and increasing (and better) use of computer-assisted assessment.

The seminal work of John Biggs (2003) on constructive alignment has led to a stronger focus on linking assessment directly to appropriate learning outcomes and ensuring these links are clear to students and markers alike. National imperatives in the UK, Australasia and elsewhere have also led to closer articulation of levels of achievement through benchmarking statements and competence frameworks.

'I know my stuff – isn't that enough?'

Staff are appointed on the basis of their expertise and experience in the subject matter of their particular disciplines. Usually, even staff new to teaching in higher education have already had at least *some* experience of working with students, for example when alongside researching or studying for higher degrees. However, when teaching first becomes a significant part of one's career it can seem rather daunting a prospect, either when stepping up to the podium in a large lecture theatre or taking home a big pile of students' work to mark.

Most of the people around you may seem to have been teaching for ever, and glide effortlessly (it appears) through the processes of preparing lectures, planning tutorials and seminars, and assessing students' work. But all of them are likely to have learned that knowing one's stuff is only a relatively small part of being able to help students to learn one's stuff!

Even more scary, the stuff you know backwards is quite unlikely to be at the heart of the material you will need to be able to teach. It is very likely that at least some of the syllabus content will be new even to you, and you may be surprised how long it can take to put together (for example) a lecture on a topic you've never studied directly before.

More often than not, you'll find someone who will be a real help. You may be set up with a mentor – an experienced colleague to guide you through those first teaching experiences. Or you may be taking over a course or a class from someone else who is still around to show you how it has been done in the past. But sometimes, you may find yourselves stepping into the shoes of someone who's moved on to a different institution or even retired. It can be scary to take on an established course or module when there's no-one around to answer your frequent questions of "What can I do when … ?"

You may already have the opportunity of relevant staff development or training. Through this, you may know those people to ask when you have worries or problems. That said, even when such training is available, you are quite likely to have to get started in your teaching *before* the training covers what you need, and then later you will need to continue to make your teaching work long after such training is completed. In either case we hope this book will help, and not least the sections which address those frequently asked 'What can I do when … ?' questions.

Teaching smarter to retain your students

Senior management often regard retention as a high institutional priority and there are often teams of staff in a university or college dedicated to monitoring institutional statistics and ensuring the lowest possible rate of dropping out.

As an individual lecturer, there is plenty you can do to contribute to student retention and this section is designed to provide hints and pointers on how you can prevent unacceptable levels of student attrition.

What kinds of student are more at risk of dropping out than others?

It is possible to identify students in high risk categories, although not all students who drop out belong to these groups and not all of these groups are necessarily at risk of dropping out. However, research tells us that there is a higher risk of students failing to complete if they:

- come from a family where there is no tradition of higher education, so they don't have the 'cultural capital' to know the rules of the game;
- are leaving foster care or are otherwise, what is termed in the jargon, a 'looked after' child (somewhat a misnomer as they are neither children nor frequently particularly well cared for);
- come from particular ethnic minority groups, for example Afro-Caribbean or Bangladeshi males;
- are from disadvantaged social groups with low family incomes;
- are registered disabled or have severe health problems;
- are studying in a country other than the one in which they grew up.

Indicative behaviours of students at risk of dropping out

Higher and further education colleges have identified a number of indicators that are linked with high levels of student attrition (see particularly Yorke, 1999). These include:

- poor (or non-) attendance;
- failing to hand in assignments on time (or at all);
- failing to return library books;
- social isolation and failing to make friends;
- frequent returns home at weekends in term time (particularly if a boyfriend/girlfriend is left behind);
- homesickness;
- unhappiness with residential accommodation;
- getting lost on campus;
- timetable confusion;
- chronic disorganisation.

With high student numbers especially, it can be difficult for any individual teacher to recognise these indicators in every single student. However, it is particularly important for you to be vigilant in the crucial early period of the first six weeks of the first semester of the first year, which Yorke (1999) identifies as crucial to retention.

A ten-point plan for retaining your students

As an individual teacher, you can:

1. *Contribute to student induction activities.* It can be helpful, as a minimum, to:
   - keep a supply of campus and local maps and transport leaflets to hand out
   - not rush away from classes as soon as they are finished

- provide leaflets on study skills, plagiarism, student support, and so on.

2 *Learn your students' names*. Everything you can do that helps to avoid students feeling alienated and alone is likely to be helpful to student retention. This includes trying to learn as many students' names as possible and using those names at every opportunity.

3 *Build in study skills guidance in to your sessions*. Many argue that short, localised bursts of study advice have more impact than larger, generic study skills sessions. You could, for example, stop mid-lecture and ask students to look at the notes made by the person sitting next to them and then to generate a short discussion on what good notes look like and the differences between note taking and note making. Similarly, for the first assignment of the course you could get students in groups to peer review early drafts of essays, and provide a helpdesk function to clarify queries from students about formats, referencing and plagiarism.

4 *Provide lots of formative feedback early on in a course or programme*. Students often feel out of their depth when they start a programme of advanced study and need reassurance that they are working along the right lines. Even mini-quizzes or short, computer-based tests which include feedback on why an answer is right or wrong can be really helpful. Excessive early summative assessment should be avoided, since vulnerable students might find a poor early mark just the evidence they need to confirm their suspicions that they don't belong at college.

5 *Help students build friendships that will enable the building of peer support*. In curriculum terms this means incorporating group tasks and activities that encourage students to mix, and making space in the timetable early in the academic year for times when students can just sit and chat informally. You can use techniques, like cross-overs, to systematically mix up students so that they work in several different groupings within a single session. However, be cautious about breaking up existing support systems. For example, international students may group together by nation so they can help each other with language issues: you may wish to enable these existing support mechanisms to be supplemented rather than replaced by new ones. Foster extra-curricular opportunities so that students feel they are members of an organisation rather than just attendees at a place of learning. Retention can be fostered by offering sporting, cultural and social opportunities outside the formal learning experiences where students can engage with staff and one another informally.

6 *Communicate regularly*. Staff at Glasgow's Caledonian University have found that follow-up phone calls to students with poor attendance resulted in significant reductions in drop out. Regular emails to the whole cohort providing bite-sized advice, tips and course information can help students feel they are 'in the

loop'. Many institutions are increasingly exploring how SMS (short messaging service) text messaging can keep students well informed about hand-in dates and other course information, and it's also possible to have automated follow-up texts to students who have not submitted work on time.

7 *Make yourself known and available to students*. This does not mean keeping a permanently open office door (although in the first six weeks of the first semester well-publicised 'office hours' can be very helpful to first year students). However, getting out and about on campus and taking part in extra-curricular activities of the kinds you encourage your students to take part in will help. Some institutions keen on retention are starting to allocate personal tutors at the application stage, who then keep responsibility for that student until graduation to ensure continuity. Another way of making yourself known is to direct students to your section of the institutional webpage, illustrated with a friendly-looking photo (not the standard departmental mug shot!) and sufficient personal information to make you come across as a real person.

8 *Brief yourself about factors influencing student retention*. Mantz Yorke's (1999) work is an excellent starting point for general information about attrition, but you could also familiarise yourself with local data by consulting national comparative data (in the UK this is provided by the Higher Education Statistics Agency (HESA): see http://www.hesa.ac.uk/) and talking to experts in your college or university who can advise you about what action is being taken in-house.

9 *Know when and where to refer on students when you personally are not competent to help them*. You should familiarise yourself early on with student support services, drug-misuse advice facilities, disability officers, counselling and other relevant services. Some institutions have specially designated Help-zones or student liaison officers who should be able to support your efforts to retain students.

10 *Recognise when you are unable to do anything to prevent drop-out*. Some students will drop out whatever a university or college does for them and we sometimes need to recognise this and let them move on.

Professionalism in practice: the challenges

Teaching smarter in the twenty-first century provides many challenges: to recruit, teach, motivate, support, assess and retain ever more diverse and demanding students, ensuring they use all their talents to the full and achieve their maximum potential, to keep abreast of new approaches in a complex and challenging environment and to cope with changing priorities in varied contexts. These are the challenges that this book sets out to equip you to address.

2

Beyond learning cycles and styles

This chapter addresses the following questions:

- Why do we need to move beyond earlier thinking about learning cycles and learning styles?
- How can we address, in our teaching, factors which underpin successful learning?
- How does 'emotional intelligence' bear upon good teaching?
- Why do we need to ensure we communicate with our learners through a variety of channels?
- How can I know whether my teaching is 'excellent'?
- How can my students demonstrate excellent *learning?*

Introduction

Making teaching work is all about making learning happen. Coffield et al. (2004) offer a penetrating critical review of many of the theories and models based on learning cycles and learning styles, and Race (2005) advocates that successful learning can be regarded as being underpinned by five straightforward factors:

- Wanting to learn – this is the same thing as 'intrinsic motivation' but there is no need to use such elitist terminology, as learners find it much easier to recognise the differences between 'need' and 'want'.
- Taking ownership of the need to learn and accepting and setting targets and goalposts – could be called 'extrinsic motivation' but there is again no need for such terminology.
- Learning by doing – practice, trial and error, repetition, experimenting.
- Learning through feedback, and being cue-conscious with feed-forward.
- Making sense of what is being learned – reflecting, digesting, turning information into knowledge.

Race (2005) goes on to suggest that these five factors do not operate in a cycle, but continuously affect each other in the same sort of way as ripples bouncing backwards and forwards when the water in a pond is disturbed by dropping in a pebble. In other words, all five of these factors can affect and enhance each other. Learning is far from being so simple that it can be 'mechanised' into sequential steps.

Teaching with emotional intelligence

Daniel Goleman described emotional intelligence as 'The capacity for recognising our own feelings and those of others, for motivating ourselves, and for managing emotions well in ourselves and in our relationships' (Goleman, 1998: 319). Alan Mortiboys (2005) advocates a series of steps by which teachers can consciously set out to develop emotionally intelligent approaches, to ensure that learning is successful.

Mortiboys suggests that teaching with emotional intelligence means:

1. planning for the emotional environment;
2. planning for the physical experience of learners;
3. dealing with your learners' expectations;
4. acknowledging individual learners;
5. listening to your learners;
6. reading and responding to the feelings of individuals and groups;
7. responding to learners' comments and questions;
8. developing self-awareness as a teacher;
9. recognising your prejudices and preferences;
10. checking your non-verbal communication;
11. acknowledging and handling your feelings as a teacher;
12. revealing your feelings to learners.

We suggest that in our bid to make teaching work, these 12 aspects form a valuable basis for designing our teaching to be responsive to learners. In other words, the 'human' dimensions of teaching are at least as important as subject mastery, the design of teaching-learning resources, and teaching techniques.

VARK: four dimensions of learning

The 'VARK' model of learning has been developed by Neil Fleming in New Zealand over many years, causing many thousands of teachers and learners to interrogate their own approaches to learning in terms of four overlapping dimensions: visual, auditory, read-write and kinaesthetic.

1. visual – maps, flowcharts, pictures, cartoons, illustrations;
2. auditory – to do with sound, tone of voice, music, emphasis as heard in spoken briefings;

3 read-write – words on paper in books, articles, magazines, newspapers, handouts, or words on-screen in e-learning environments;
4 kinaesthetic – to do with movement, motion, gesture, dance, practical skills, physical activities.

These four dimensions of learning can be regarded as channels of communication between learners and the whole of the learning environment surrounding them, including teachers. As Fleming's work illustrates, people vary considerably in terms of which of these channels work best for them. Moreover, this is by no means fixed, and people vary day to day and year to year in their responses to these channels. Making teaching work therefore should necessarily involve us in considering how best to ensure that we are 'broadcasting' on all of these channels wherever possible, to maximise the learning across any group of learners. It is of particular interest to extend consideration of these dimensions to the field of assessment – in other words, how we attempt to measure the results of learning (for details of this model, visit www.vark-learn.com).

Teaching to make learning happen

Bearing in mind the human aspects of teaching as identified by Mortiboys, and the channels of communication as identified by Fleming, we suggest that making teaching work can be addressed systematically by paying attention also to the five underpinning factors in the 'ripples' model advocated by Race (2005).

You can consciously set out to help your learners to *want* to learn. This links to sharing with learners the benefits they will derive from learning successfully – addressing for them the question of 'What's in it for me?' You should think purposefully about the human side of your relationship with learners, so that they engage with you and believe in you as a teacher.

You can also purposefully set out to help your learners take ownership of their need to learn. You can do this by spelling out clearly the intended learning outcomes, so that students know exactly what they should be aiming to achieve in order to demonstrate that they have learned successfully. When learners can see the targets clearly, they are in a much better position to work systematically towards demonstrating their achievement of the intended learning outcomes.

Since learning-by-doing is so critically important, teaching necessarily involves planning very carefully what learners are intended to do along each learning pathway. You need to be thinking of how best you can engage them in practice, repetition and experimentation. In particular, it is important to ensure that opportunities for learning through trial and error are available, and that learning from mistakes is made attractive rather than threatening.

Feedback remains a vital step in learning – particularly feed-forward or feed-ahead – so that learners can continuously fine-tune their learning-by-doing using feedback from their teachers. Later in this book, we give detailed suggestions regarding the various ways and means whereby you can ensure that your learners make the most of a wide range of feedback processes.

Helping your learners to make sense of what they are learning is probably the most important dimension of effective teaching. You can't, however, do the 'making sense' steps for your learners – you can only strive to set up environments and conditions to maximise the opportunities they have to make sense of what they are learning, particularly by addressing the 'wanting and needing' dimensions, clarifying the learning-by-doing which will lead to success and ensuring that feedback is timely, helpful and motivating.

Natural human processes

Both learning and teaching can be regarded as natural human processes, as both occur throughout life and in informal social environments as well as educational settings. Emotional intelligence is very closely linked to simply being human, and as teachers we need to respond to learners as fellow human beings and to use all of our channels of communication to interact effectively with them.

The purposeful harnessing of emotional intelligence is likely to be all the more successful when we set out to apply it in ways that recognise the natural processes underpinning successful learning. We need to use our emotional intelligence to enhance learners' wanting to learn, giving them greater ownership of their need to learn and helping to structure their learning-by-doing, allowing them to make the most of feedback not only from us but from each other. Cumulatively, this is likely to have optimum pay-off in terms of helping our learners to make sense of the subject-matter they are studying, and to respond to whichever combination of visual, auditory, read-write and kinaesthetic channels that work best for each individual learner.

Overall, the human dimensions of teaching and learning are much more significant than any particular learning preferences our learners may believe that they have, as teaching with emotional intelligence embraces the use of all of the natural channels of communication identified by Fleming in his VARK instrument in order to reach all of our learners.

Towards 'excellent' teaching

What is 'excellent' teaching? Is 'excellent' an appropriate word to apply to something so multi-faceted as teaching? There is always the danger when trying to 'measure' quality that we end up measuring things that lend themselves to measurement but which aren't actually really important. Yet excellent teaching does exist, and any student is likely to have a pretty good idea about who is a really excellent teacher in their experience – and who isn't!

At first sight, it might be argued that excellent teaching must be evidenced by excellent learning. In other words, the level of achievement of students may provide an indicator of excellent teaching. But it is not as simple as this, as the students may already have achieved their excellent learning in spite of the teaching they experience. 'Value added' is a further consideration: the teacher whose students travel far in their achievement may be teaching more excellently than the teacher whose students already have the potential to achieve highly.

Breaking down the meaning of 'excellent teaching' from a student point of view is a multi-faceted business. You may find it useful to run through the table below, trying to gauge what would be your students' responses to these indicators of excellent teaching, ticking 'Definitely' if your are sure you are making them feel like this about their learning, 'Perhaps' if this may sometimes be the case – or 'Afraid not!' if you feel your teaching isn't yet working quite so well against some of these indicators. Better still, ask the students themselves.

What do your students think about the way you teach?

My students know they have been on the receiving end of excellent teaching when:

Some indicators of excellent teaching from a student point of view	***Definitely***	***Perhaps***	***Afraid not!***
I learn difficult things successfully, and the teacher makes this easier for me.			
I look forward to my next session with this teacher.			
I want to become more like the person this teacher projects.			
What I already knew is celebrated, built upon, and valued, by this teacher.			
I feel good about the learning, because I feel good about the teacher.			
I feel I can talk openly to the teacher, even if I never do talk.			
The learning is made manageable for me, a bit at a time.			
The teacher makes the targets clear, and helps me to see what is in it for me to reach them.			
Even when in a large class, I feel I am being responded to as an individual by this teacher.			

Some indicators of excellent teaching from a student point of view	***Definitely***	***Perhaps***	***Afraid not!***
The teacher is enthusiastic about the subject – even passionate about it.			
This teacher, when marking my work, gives me feedback in a sensitive and caring way.			
The feedback always includes suggestions about how I can build on my strengths and bring them to bear on improving my next piece of work.			
If I don't attend one of this teacher's sessions, I really miss something; just getting the notes or the handouts doesn't compensate for the learning experience I lose, so I aim not to miss any sessions from this teacher.			
Each session with this teacher feels like a learning experience, and not just a lecture or tutorial.			
I feel ownership of the success of my learning – at the end of the day I feel that I have done it myself.			
The learning is made relevant to me, to my world, to my work.			
I develop as a learner with this teacher, alongside learning the subject.			
I am never put down, nor allowed to feel small, nor feel that any question I ask would be seen as silly or trivial – even when it is.			
I admire and respect the teacher, and wanted to be more like this person.			
The teacher seems to care for me as a human being, not just as a learner.			
I feel that the teacher is on my side, even at those times when the learning is a struggle.			
The teacher doesn't condemn me when I just can't do it.			
I feel that there is a warm, personal relationship between the teacher and myself.			
I continue to want to learn more from this teacher.			

Aim to use your enthusiasm to be inspirational!

Possibly the most pleasant feedback that any teacher can be given is that their enthusiasm was inspirational to their students. Enthusiasm is infectious, and closely related to inspiring students. Lack of enthusiasm is infectious too however! The following suggestions may help you to transmit some of your own enthusiasm to your students – and help you to hide your lack of enthusiasm when necessary!

Ten ways to transmit your enthusiasm to your students

1 *Take notice of trends from student feedback.* Most course evaluation questionnaires hesitate to probe into students' feelings about the enthusiasm (or lack of it) demonstrated by their lecturers or tutors. However, in open-ended responses on such questionnaires, students often comment favourably about particular lecturers being enthusiastic, passionate, dedicated, and the like. These comments are almost always positive ones about teaching. The reverse occurs sometimes as well, when poorer teaching is linked to lecturers seeming bored with the topic themselves, and so on. So it could be argued that your enthusiasm as demonstrated through your teaching is closely aligned to indicators of your teaching quality – at least in students' minds.

2 *Be enthusiastic about the subject.* You probably are already, or you wouldn't be teaching it! This may be true to some extent, but in every subject there are some favourite areas and other parts one just can't summon up much enthusiasm for. But when students detect you're teaching a dull part of a subject, they are likely to register it quickly as dull to them too. This can require a bit of role playing on your part. Alternatively, it can help to face up to some elements of study being 'rites of passage' but do make it really clear that these are absolute necessities and will lead on to much more interesting ground.

3 *Be enthusiastic about students!* Students are quick to detect any lack of respect for them. If you're so involved in your own research that teaching feels like a tedious chore, it is not surprising that students aren't inspired. The most successful teachers *like* working with students – or at least are very convincing at seeming to do so.

4 *Be enthusiastic about the course or module.* This can sometimes be harder to achieve, especially if you're not the designer. However, any real or implied criticisms of the curriculum you make can seriously undermine students' confidence regarding the learning experience they are getting. When you have genuine reservations about the curriculum it is best for you to work hard behind the scenes towards making it better in future, but to continue to contribute to your teaching work as though you really like it.

5 *Be enthusiastic about colleagues and their work.* This is sometimes harder still! However, students are extremely receptive to any comments you make which can be interpreted as being critical of other teachers they know. This in turn can undermine their trust and confidence in their learning from those other teachers – or indeed if students have already developed trust in these people, it can backfire and alienate students from learning in your own teaching contexts. Refraining from any implied criticism of colleagues in teaching contexts could be considered to be a key area of acting professionally.

6 *Show enthusiasm for the department and the institution.* Even if you're looking for a job elsewhere because you've lost this enthusiasm, this is not the fault of your students. They are probably stuck there, at least for the duration of your course with them. All of us can pick faults with a department or institution which we know too well, but it is not in your students' interests for you to communicate your misgivings to them. They are there to gain a qualification from that institution, and you can only damage their motivation if you weaken their belief in that goal.

7 *Be enthusiastic about giving feedback to students.* Be enthusiastic in *helping* students to improve their work. Going that extra mile in complimenting students on excellent work can inspire them to continue to try to do really well. But don't be too enthusiastic when giving *critical* feedback.

8 *Show enthusiasm in helping students to succeed.* Part of your job as a teacher is helping students to get their act together so that they demonstrate their maximum potential in coursework assignments and exams. Show that you want to do everything you can to help them to be successful. This is *not* about dropping strong hints about forthcoming exam questions, but much more about making sure that they know how to approach their learning to guarantee their own success.

9 *Be enthusiastic about getting feedback from your students.* For example, don't just administer an end-of-module evaluation questionnaire with little enthusiasm, because you yourself don't *believe* in the questionnaire or in end-of-module feedback. In either case, collect your own feedback in your own way as well. When students feel that you really *want* their feedback, the feedback they give you is much more deeply considered.

10 *If you are already highly enthusiastic, just check that it shows!* You could ask your students – they will definitely know. Likewise, colleagues should know too.

What is 'excellent *learning*'?

Making your teaching work is, in one way or another, about causing your students to learn the subjects you are teaching them. 'Excellent learning' is about making sense of what is being learned, rather than just storing up information to regurgitate on command when answering exam questions.

A very important part of your job is to help your students become better at learning. Students need to become excellent learners so that they can go forward in their lives and careers and continue to learn and develop effectively and efficiently, even when there are no excellent teachers around.

So what can you expect from your students in terms of 'excellent learning'? As with 'excellent teaching', it is wise to regard 'excellent learning' as something which can't really be defined or measured, but to identify some qualities and actions which collectively may contribute towards it.

Ten indicators of excellent learning

Students may be engaging in 'excellent learning' when their behaviours and achievements include an appropriate mixture of the following:

1. Participating fully in lectures, tutorials, and other teaching-learning contexts.
2. Being willing, when asked, to explain how they believe their learning is progressing.
3. Accepting full responsibility for catching up on any teaching-learning sessions they are unable to attend.
4. Readily trying to ask and answer questions in teaching-learning contexts.
5. Demonstrating a caring and supportive attitude towards their fellow-students.
6. Undertaking specific preparatory work when briefed to prepare for lectures or tutorials.
7. Spontaneously undertaking background preparatory work, so they are not starting from scratch when starting on a curriculum that is unfamiliar to them.
8. Achieving excellent grades or scores for their coursework, and being able to explain their work to you, so that there is no doubt about the ownership of their work.
9. Demonstrating achievement which exceeds the standards of the intended learning outcomes.
10. Giving useful feedback, when invited, on their experience of each teaching, learning and assessment element of their programme.

Helping your students to take charge of the factors underpinning their learning

We end this chapter by returning to the five underpinning factors we mentioned at the beginning. With your help students can be involved in taking charge of how these five factors work for them. You can encourage them to:

- Explore their own motivation, seeking good reasons which will fuel their *wanting* to learn – in other words, to build their own rationale for *why* they are learning, and what they want to *become* as a result of their learning.
- Clarify exactly what they *need* to learn – in other words, to identify exactly what they need to become able to do as a result of their learning by taking ownership of the real purpose of the intended learning outcomes involved.
- Recognise that *learning-by-doing* is how it all happens in practice, which encourages them to put their energy into practice, repetition, trial and error and so on.
- Accept that *making sense* of what is being learned is important, and thereby to try harder to *digest* information, selecting from it the really useful parts rather than just collecting and attempting to store as much information as possible.
- Make the most of *feedback* on their learning from all possible sources – from each other, from teachers or trainers, from books and articles, from anyone else who can give them feedback on their actions, their evidence, their *making sense* and so on.

Students find it perfectly understandable that the actions listed above all affect and enhance each other, and that any combination (or indeed all) of the actions can be happening at any given moment during their learning.

Significant learning takes place without any teaching, training, instructing, or tutoring processes. The phrase 'self-taught' is in widespread use where individuals have reached outstanding levels of achievement without teaching interventions. It could be said that the people concerned have simply found their own ways of mastering how they learn, and have developed their own ways to address the factors described above.

Imagine you yourself needed to learn something new, and that there was no one to help you to learn it. Imagine you found yourself in a library, surrounded by books, articles, videos, web-access and so on – in other words, adrift in a sea of information about the topic. This taxes the imagination rather weakly, because most people have been there already! What do you do about it? What does work is starting to *process* all that information – to find out what the important parts really are, what they mean, and then to rearrange the information. You may learn by doing – namely practice, repetition, trial and error. You may reduce the vast sea of information down to manageable proportions – by summarising it. You may try to get feedback on how your learning is going. Gradually, you will digest and make sense of the information.

Perhaps, therefore, in a bid to make your teaching work you may need to spend much more time helping your students to see how learning really happens. Developing students' control of their learning is, of course, already happening under a variety of labels – 'key skills', 'transferable skills', and so on. But possibly because we so often use the word 'skills' for such things, people don't yet quite realise that these are exactly the 'skills' which underpin even the most sophisticated levels of knowledge or understanding. Perhaps the most important outcome of any element of learning is that of becoming a better *learner* bit by bit. So making teaching work is more than making learning happen – it's also about making learners better at learning for themselves.

3

Supporting individual learning and responding to learning needs

This chapter addresses the following questions:

- What is wrong with student learning?
- How can we respond to individual learning needs more efficiently and effectively?
- How can we introduce inclusive practice and support special learning needs?

The need for smarter approaches to supporting learning

The recent and rapid increase in the number of students entering higher education has resulted in large student cohorts. These cohorts are typically drawn from many nationalities and from varied social, cultural and religious backgrounds, and include students of varied physical and cognitive abilities. Universities now need to respond to the challenge of educating and supporting these large numbers of diverse students. In some cases, teacher contact with students is now restricted to delivering to large classes, whilst support is provided by student liaison officers separated from the actual learning and teaching environment. As many teachers find themselves increasingly distanced from their students, it is perhaps unsurprising that higher education is suffering from a problem with student retention. We need to rethink how we may more effectively and more efficiently support the individual learning of the diverse range of students in higher education today.

What's wrong with student learning?

There is a problem in the UK with student achievement, neatly summed up by Yorke and Longden:

> It is probable that there is more academic failure in UK higher education than there should be. There seems to be scope in institutions for improving the ways in which they support students' learning – and hence for reducing the incidence of academic failure. (Yorke and Longden, 2004: 39)

For several years educational developers have accepted that student learning is best supported through a constructive alignment of learning outcomes, methods and assessment. The specification of learning outcomes is undeniably useful to course designers and external examiners and there has been an enormous effort over the last couple of decades to redesign the UK's higher education curriculum in terms of learning outcomes. Different learning environments will foster different types of learning and those learning environments conducive to deep learning enable learners to select appropriate approaches for given tasks and to move beyond a knowledge of facts.

However, students today commonly adopt surface learning. This is an understandable response to a teaching environment which fails to encourage them to adopt a deep approach. Boud (1990) suggests that assessment tasks typically encourage a narrow approach to learning that focuses on reproducing that which is presented at the expense of independent activity. Knight and Yorke (2003) refer to this fostering of 'learned dependence' where the student does not seek to go beyond the boundaries set by the tutor. This dependence we have created between students and tutors may well pose challenges to student learning, as it is at odds with the desire to prepare students for lifelong learning and the need to allow students to learn how to learn independently.

What are we doing wrong?

Student-centred learning should start with the needs of the student rather than the demands of the subject and yet we focus so much of our time on preparing materials, on delivery and on marking work which students often don't collect. This time could be more effectively used to identify individual learning needs and to develop students as autonomous learners by providing a learning environment that encourages students to explore, experiment and reflect. So how can you do this?

Work towards an integrated approach to supporting individual learning

Students, typically, have to deal with a large range of advisors including tutors, learning support officers, technicians and administrators and may be unsure exactly who to contact in a particular situation. There is often a large team supporting different aspects of a student's learning experience and it is sensible to consider whether the system can be streamlined and made easier for students to gain the support they need. Consider the system from your student's point of view. There may be advantages for that student in geographically locating the learning support team together. It is clearly important that all those involved in the support of students communicate efficiently and anything that can be done to facilitate easier communication should be considered.

Give learning support officers access to academic notes, materials and assignments prior to class and consider involving administrative staff in assessing students' problems and needs. It is useful to coach both staff and students on regulations and procedures so that the advice given to students is consistent, and to make documentation available online to allow document sharing. You could also set up a mentor bank or expert directory, so that students (and staff) know where to go for help and advice.

A seamless approach to technology can be challenging and it is becoming increasingly important to work closely with technical support staff when designing programmes. The pace of change in technology is fast and we need to stay ahead (or at least abreast!) of students in terms of technical knowledge. Technical staff may be able to work with you to develop online materials and effectively utilise virtual learning environments. They may also be able to input very positively to programme design by identifying opportunities to incorporate and exploit mobile phones, MP3 players and other digital media. Many institutions are looking to offer 24 hour support to students, with the extended opening of libraries and technical support being available (online and on campus) to support printing and so on.

Reduce the time you spend on preparation and delivery of lectures and learning objects

The lecture remains a standard event on many programmes, even though it can be a relatively ineffective and inefficient teaching method. Many lecturers devote hours to preparing new lectures and the conscientious can invest almost equal amounts of time updating lecture material for each subsequent delivery. In the past the lecture was a principal opportunity for students to gain information and quite rightly lectures were valued as forums for the sharing of knowledge. In the current age of information overload there is far less need for the lecture. However, ironically, many academic staff find themselves spending longer than ever on lecture preparation. This is, at least, partially a result of the increased expectations of students today who require polished professional presentations with illustrated handouts.

Given the plethora of learning resources now available, you should think about whether you really need lectures or whether it would be more efficient and effective for your students to access content via electronic or other learning resources. However, beware that you don't simply transfer the time you currently invest in preparing lectures to preparing electronic learning resources and other learning objects. There are so many high quality learning resources freely available now, through the UK's Higher Education Academy subject centres and from university websites worldwide, that there is often little need to prepare bespoke materials for each programme.

Redesign your assessment, learning and teaching practice to support regular, and ideally individual, formative feedback with students

Your irreplaceable value as a teacher is to be found in dialogue with students. Prioritise opportunities for dialogue and feedback in the student timetable. It is generally accepted that formative feedback about performance and attainment is necessary for effective learning to occur. Feed-forward regarding the steps required to improve current performance is particularly important in facilitating effective learning and it's a good idea to check that feed-forward is actually being given, rather than simply feedback on what has already been done. It is also important to help students to identify feed-forward, and build upon it.

The most successful formative feedback and feed-forward:

- are immediate and regular;
- enhance learning during learning;
- should be used to empower students as self-regulated learners;
- can only make a difference if students have the skills and knowledge to act upon it.

This last point is often overlooked. Sadler argues that it is important that learners possess a concept of the standard being aimed for.

> A key premise is that for students to be able to improve, they must develop the capacity to monitor the quality of their own work during actual production, rather than later on. This in turn requires that students possess an appreciation of what high quality work is, that they have the evaluative skill necessary for them to compare with some objectivity the quality of what they are producing in relation to the higher standard, and that they develop a store of tactics or moves which can be drawn upon to modify their own work. (Sadler, 1989: 119)

Formative feedback should be an integral part of learning, but the constraints of contact time in higher education and student expectations often result in teachers prioritising the delivery of content and summative assessment.

Reduce the time you spend marking

Think about redesigning assessments so that marking is less time-consuming. Consider computer-aided or computer-based assessment or whether other stakeholders could be involved in marking. Are you over assessing? If you find that a significant amount of your time is being focused on marking, administration and related activities such as plagiarism detection, then you need to question whether and how this time is supporting student learning. Is it worth spending time differentiating between a mark of 53 per cent and a mark of 56 per cent in the first stages of a programme? How does this benefit the student? Design your marking schemes with efficiency in mind and keep the assessment process as simple as possible.

Invest time in getting to know your students

Yorke and Longden (2004) as well as others have highlighted how important it is to make every student feel 'part of the programme' while studying. Your students will take more notice of you if they feel that they know you – and above all – that you know them. People in general tend to take more notice of people they know. This is particularly important when you work with small groups of students, as they are much more likely to expect you to know who they are! Getting their names right is a useful step towards building up the sort of relationship which fosters learning, and which reduces the risk of drop out. The following suggestions adapted from Race (2006) provide some general advice on how to improve your 'hit rate' of correct name-calling in your teaching.

- *Use sticky labels.* At early stages it's useful to give students sticky labels to write their names on in bold felt-tip pen, even in quite large groups. At the beginning of the course, ask students 'What do you want to be called?' This gives you the chance to call them by the name they prefer – and gives them the chance to start getting to know each other.
- *Learn all the easy names first.* If you have a group with three Peters in, make sure you know them first and which one is which! You then have (say) a three in twenty chance of getting someone's first name right!
- *Take particular care with difficult names.* If you have a name that you find diffi-

cult or unusual to say, write it out clearly and check how to say it, then write it phonetically in a way you will recognise over the top. Use the name as often as you can until you've mastered it, regularly checking that you've got it right.

- *Consider students' feelings.* Think how you feel when someone gets your name wrong – especially someone you would have expected to know it. One of the problems with university teaching is that new students can feel quite anonymous and alone, especially when part of a large class.
- *Help students to learn each others' names.* In groups with up to about 20 students, try the following round: 'Tell us your name, and tell us something about your name.' This can be a good icebreaker, and can be very memorable too, helping people to develop associative links with the names involved.
- *Help students to get to know each other better.* An alternative round is to get the students sitting in a circle. Ask one to say his or her name, then the person to their left to say 'I am ... and this is ... .' Carry on round the circle, adding one name at each stage, till someone goes right round the circle correctly. A further alternative is to ask students to introduce themselves individually, stating their names first, and then two of their 'likes' and 'dislikes', so that some memorable details help associate that person with their name.
- *Use your list of names to quiz students.* To help you get to know their names, once you have a complete list of these ask people from your list at random some (easy) questions, not to catch them out but to help you to put names to faces.
- *Consider using place cards.* In places where small groups of students are sitting in particular places for a while, it is useful to give them each a 'place card' (a folded A5 sheet of card serves well) and to write their name on both sides of the card and place the card in front of them. Cards can be seen at a distance much better than labels. This allows you to address individuals by name, and also helps them to get to know each other.

Invest time in listening to your students

Here you should focus on individual student perceptions. There is a growing recognition of the need to prioritise student perceptions of their learning experiences, so that these can be matched with the teaching that is offered. The issue of the alignment of perceptions and practices is highly relevant to all higher education institutions, particularly those at the forefront of widening participation and internationalisation.

We need to take a personal approach to supporting student learning, and personal tutoring or academic coaching is common in many institutions. The academic coach typically provides individual academic guidance, whilst a personal tutor role may additionally encompass pastoral care. Higher Education can learn from the model of personal tutoring and coaching found in many parts of F.E. There is much to be gained from one-to-one discussion giving students tailored feedback, direction and motivation and sharing knowledge, best practice and expertise. It is particularly important to understand and react to student need at transition points such as induction.

Invest your time in developing students as autonomous, self-regulated learners early on in their course

The first six weeks of a programme represent a significant period in the student learning experience and in forming student attitudes to learning. There are huge pay-offs for us and for students if we equip them for independent learning at the beginning of their higher education experience. By doing so, students will be able to exploit and act upon formative feedback and be more effective learners throughout their programmes.

The challenge facing academics looking to develop students as autonomous learners is how to embed skills for learning into the early stages of a programme. It is particularly important in the first weeks of the student experience, to consider giving students instant formative feedback. Support students to move away from a model of 'learned dependence', which they may have experienced prior to coming into higher education, by designing tasks that encourage and credit students for experimenting and for failing. Provide informative student assignment briefs that are not too prescriptive and keep the system of assessment as simple as possible. Optimise opportunities for one-to-one and small group discussions about learning in the context of a particular task or module activity.

Involve students as partners in assessment, research and course development

There is potentially much to be gained from a mutually supportive relationship between teachers and students. Empower the learner to shape their own learning experience and think about how students can help you with your workload. Think about whether it is feasible and desirable to pass more control to the individual student for their learning and assessment. You could also consider allowing students to have more input into their curriculum design. Why not introduce students to research at the beginning rather than in the latter stages of their programmes?

Some of the benefits of working in partnership with students in research include the following:

- Research may foster an attitude of inquiry.
- Tutor-student collaboration may help a teacher to identify with their students' learning.
- Students can develop transferable skills, such as critical analysis and the presentation of findings.
- The outputs may be able to inform the curriculum.

There has long been a debate about ownership of the curriculum – to what extent should the curriculum be determined by those who teach, and to what extent and in what ways should others influence the development and evaluation of a curriculum? A question which is asked less regularly is to what extent should students own the said curriculum? Clearly this will be largely dependent upon discipline, but in every context where busy teachers are trying to balance research with teaching it may be worth considering the advantages and practicalities of developing students' research skills at the earliest possible opportunity in a course, to improve their learning experience and to exploit the potential for teacher-learner collaboration through research.

Address special educational needs

You need to ensure that diverse students are able to engage with learning on an equal basis and you also need to make adjustments to enable students with special needs to participate fully in learning. In response to the UK's SENDA (Special Educational Needs and Disabilities Act) 2001 requirements that no learner should be disadvantaged because of special educational needs, most higher education institutions in the UK now provide significant support to students with physical impairment, mental health needs, illness and communication difficulties – including visually impaired, auditory impaired students and learners with dyslexia. Whilst it is always advisable to take advice on what an individual student needs in terms of support, there are also adjustments you can look to make to your teaching practice.

Five of the key reasonable adjustments when teaching students with special educational needs are:

- Making use of disabled students to advise on inclusive practice. The likelihood is that the majority of disabled students already have successful study strategies prior to coming to university, and they will also know where pitfalls and problems are likely to arise in assignments for students with similar impairments to their own.
- Making best use of a university's disability officers and other informed colleagues to build a knowledge base on the needs of disabled students.

- Ensuring that materials are accessible in a range of media and reducing the length of time it may take to make accessible materials available.
- Recognising that students on the whole are extremely supportive of disabled students, but may need reminding of simple things like facing the student with hearing impairment when addressing the group as a whole. Ideally, let the student concerned identify for fellow students what is the most helpful behaviour.
- Exploring the uses of assistive technologies. In the UK, TechDis (www.TechDis.ac.uk) is a national resource advising higher education and further education practitioners on a wide range of assistive technologies for disabled students. (Adapted from Pickford and Brown, 2006)

Address social diversity

You need to be cautious about assuming that your own norms are universal. You may find the following suggestions useful when teaching a socially diverse class.

Following are five suggestions for ensuring an equivalence of experience for diverse students:

- Clarify expectations about what is expected in terms of originality. In some cultures, including the ideas and even the precise original words of the teacher within assessed tasks is an expectation rather than something to be criticised, and a lack of shared understandings about this can lead to problems if not addressed early on.
- Be inclusive in terms of cultural references in case study material. Don't always use examples from the home nation and avoid excessive references to cultural stereotypes.
- Avoid implying that all students are part of a particular age group when making cultural/social references that may marginalise older or younger students.
- Think about the language you use in giving feedback. Jargon or slang might be incomprehensible or confusing to someone who doesn't share your first language. Irony rarely translates well, so is best avoided in oral feedback.
- Be sensitive about religious festival dates. This should be considered at the outset rather than having to make last minute arrangements. There may be implications, for example, if students are expected to undertake gruelling lengthy assignments at times when they are likely to be fasting. (Adapted from Pickford and Brown, 2006)

In terms of making teaching work, the most important thing to do is to build in adjustments when a programme is designed. It is neither cost-effective nor sensible to wait for problems to present themselves and then to provide support for individual students at the eleventh hour. It is far better to ensure that we think about alternatives right from the start.

Conclusion

The nature of the learning experience in higher education today has been radically affected by changes in widening participation, funding and the pace of technological change. In exploring how best to be inclusive, many higher education institutions in the UK have sensibly aimed to implement approaches that not only avoid discriminatory behaviour but also demonstrate good practice for all students. The effort that you put into ensuring inclusive practice will (hopefully) reduce the amount of time you will need to invest in making adjustments on an ad hoc basis throughout the programme.

You can only support individual learning effectively if you free up time from preparation, delivery and marking. The burden of transmitting knowledge can, and has to be, transferred to other media. Teacher time should be focused on dialogue, formative feedback, and on supporting student exploration. If you are to focus on formative feedback and the facilitation of effective learning, you may need to re-engineer your entire approach to curriculum design, assessment and teaching practices. To make teaching work you should see modules as integrated sets of learning opportunities, with face-to-face and resource-based components working together and reinforcing each other. You may need to rethink your relationship with your students and look to new ways that you can work together and be more flexible in your approaches to assessment, teaching and learning.

4

Working with small groups

This chapter addresses the following questions:

- What do we mean by 'small groups' and why should we work with them?
- How can we work with small groups in the classroom?
- How can we motivate students through seminars and tutorials?
- How can we effectively design teamwork?
- What do we need to know about group behaviours?

Introduction

With drives towards efficiency and cost-effective provision, in some disciplines small-group teaching has been reduced or even phased out in favour of lectures and resource-based learning (paper-based, online, or both). This is a great shame because groupwork has great potential, if well designed and managed, to enhance student learning. Perhaps the most significant reasons for using small-group teaching are the benefits students acquire which lie beyond the curriculum. The *emergent* learning outcomes associated with small groupwork help students to equip themselves with the skills and attitudes they will need for each of the next stages of their careers – and lives.

The range of contexts in which you are likely to work with small groups is broad and includes:

- Tutor led small-group classes such as tutorials, seminars and problem-based learning.
- Student led small groups or teams such as project teams, student led seminars and learning sets.
- Syndicate groupings within larger classes.
- Virtual or online groups.

There is often a lack of student engagement in small-group work and in the availability of time and other resources to support small-group work. In this chapter, we will discuss factors which are important in determining the success of small groups both within and outside the classroom, and suggest steps you can take to support effective student learning in small groups efficiently.

What could go wrong if there was no small-group teaching?

If small-group teaching for some reason had to be discontinued, the following manifestations could occur:

- Increased drop out and failure statistics, because students would not have enough opportunity to have help with their difficulties.
- Students would be much less aware of how well (or indeed how badly) their learning was progressing, as they would miss out on small-group contexts allowing them to gain a great deal of feedback from each other.
- More time would need to be used trying to help those students who make appointments for one-to-one help with particular problems – often the same problem many times over.
- There would be more interruptions to the flow of large-group teaching, when it would no longer be possible in a lecture to reply to a question 'this is just the right sort of question to discuss in detail in your next tutorial – bring it along then and make sure that it is sorted out to your satisfaction'.
- Increased risk of students succeeding satisfactorily in written assessment scenarios, but not having gained the level of mastery of the subject matter that comes from discussing it, arguing about it, and explaining it to other people.
- Increased risk of lecturers remaining unaware of the significant problems which students were experiencing until too late – when the problems have turned into assessment failures.

What is the tutor's role in working with small groups?

If you can get students learning in groups effectively this can be efficient, freeing you up from instruction to focus on other aspects of the learning experience. However, your role is more than that of subject expert. You need to facilitate group cohesion and support student learning. Don't assume that your students know how to work in groups. You might need to take some responsibility for how your students will learn in the small-group class and should consider building in checkpoints to monitor how the group is performing. It is as important to plan small-group learning as it is any other class. Have a clear framework deliberately planned to meet the objectives of the session and outline the intentions. You need to be aware of the aims, the appropriateness of tasks, and when to intervene. You should be clear about what students need to know and what prior experience of groupwork students have had. If this is none, then you will need to prepare them to get the most from small-group contexts.

Five ways to help students to learn well in small-group contexts

1. *Help students to* want *more strongly to learn.* Your best chance to achieve this is through your own enthusiasm for the subject – and making it obvious that you have students' best interests at heart and want them to succeed. If you seem bored with a subject, it is hardly surprising that students will not be excited by it!
2. *Help students to take ownership of their need to learn.* You can do this by reminding students of what's in it for them if they succeed with their learning, and by helping them to see exactly what they need to become able to do to succeed. This boils down to making it very clear what sort of evidence of achievement they need to be working towards. It also helps if you remind students that this is going to be perfectly manageable for them, and that even the most complex outcomes are achieved one small step at a time.
3. *Make sure students understand that learning happens by doing.* Help them to see that very little happens just sitting looking at some notes or handout materials, but that learning starts when they try to do something with the materials. Help them also to see that learning happens bit by bit, and that even the most difficult tasks can be broken down incrementally. When learning from books, handouts, or on-screen, a useful maxim is 'Not much learning will happen unless you've got a pen in your hand and are using it'. In other words, you can help students not to 'drift', but to make notes, jot down questions, practise answering questions and so on, whilst working with learning resource materials.
4. *Make sure that students get quick and useful feedback.* Help them to assess their own achievements, to reflect on things they have done successfully, to think quite deliberately about what worked in their learning and to assess why it worked. Even more importantly, you can help students to learn from their mistakes. If you help them to see that getting things wrong at first is a very productive step along the way to getting them right, they can gradually become able to look at learning by trial-and-error as a valid and productive way of going about their learning.
5. *Help students to make sense of things.* Point out the benefits of collaborative learning here. Help students to find out how much they can get their own heads round something they have just learned by explaining it to some fel-

low students who haven't yet seen the light, and then talking them through it till they too have made sense of it. It can be important not to allow students to worry too much about 'not understanding' something – especially when difficult concepts or ideas are involved. It can, in fact, be enormously comforting for students who are struggling if you say "don't worry that you don't yet understand this – just keep practising with it, and the understanding will come in its own time."

Working with small groups in the classroom

Small-group teaching between students and tutors is important for a number of reasons. Students have the opportunity to ask questions about what they have covered in lectures that they wouldn't have asked their lecturers at the time. Students can feel very isolated if they never have a chance to speak with their tutors. They can also find out a lot more about how their tutors' minds work, and equally lecturers can check up on how students' learning is going. This can be achieved by probing students' understanding and getting students to evidence their learning. In small-group classes students can also learn from each other's successes and failures. A question that one student asks in a group tutorial may be of interest to the other students, and all can learn to rely on each other to be learning resources.

And yet both tutors and students often end up frustrated by groupwork. Tutors have to learn how to teach using small groups and students have to learn how to work in small groups. The best starting point when considering working with small groups is to establish the aim of the groupwork.

Making the most of seminars and tutorials

The terms 'seminar' and 'tutorial' are sometimes used interchangeably for small-group sessions. However, strictly speaking, a *seminar* is usually meant to be a student led, small-group session, for example when one or more students gives a short presentation then answers questions and opens up discussion on a pre-assigned topic. Here, the tutor's main responsibility is to be the facilitator or chairperson.

Tutorials come in many shapes and sizes – from one-to-one, face-to-face sessions between staff and individual students to small-group, teaching-learning sessions directed largely by tutors – but with a considerable expectation of active learning by students rather than passive 'sitting and listening'. In some disciplines, tutorials often take the form of problems-classes, where small groups of students work through quantitative problems either individually or collaboratively, guided by the tutor, and helped out when necessary.

Making teaching work in seminars

A seminar is an opportunity for active learning through dialogue and exploration. Managed well, it can be transforming and can help students to make important discoveries. Done badly, however, a seminar can be an embarrassing and depressing experience. It is worth investing the time in sharing a clear sense of purpose, agreeing ground rules and planning the seminar. Seminars, whether tutor led or student led, can be an effective way for students to test out ideas. The use of student led seminars is increasing and can be an effective way both of learning and also consolidating learning. However, many students find their first seminars daunting and it is important that they are briefed on their seminar roles, supported throughout it, and given feedback.

When planning a seminar you may find it useful to:

- Consider linking the seminar to learning outcomes. Identify what the students should be able to do at the end of the seminar and ensure that your students are aware of this.
- Decide how you will assess the seminar. If the seminar presentation is to be assessed think about involving the student participants as assessors. Consider the value of basing exam questions upon issues discussed in seminars.
- Ensure the room layout is appropriate with the correct number of chairs in a circle or horseshoe (or if it is a student led seminar, allow the seminar leader to position the furniture as they wish) and that you are clear about any requirements for equipment in advance.
- Encourage the students to come up with questions about the subject matter. Formulating good questions is a valuable skill for learners.
- Clarify students' roles in a student led seminar and establish ground rules about attendance, form of presentation, participation and feedback.
- Help students if they are showing signs of distress by reassuring them, recapping or prompting them.
- Build contingency into the scheduling of seminar programmes to allow for student sickness and the like.
- Consider how feedback will be given. A student can choose when and where they read and reflect on written feedback, but immediate and public oral feedback has to be handled sensitively. It is a good idea to encourage the presenter to start the feedback with how they think the seminar went. The tutor should ideally start their oral feedback with a positive comment and specify that feed-

back from student participants should be specific and related to agreed criteria. Students could also give written feedback to the presenter after the seminar and you may consider the value of assessing the quality of this feedback.

Ten ways to motivate your students to participate actively in seminars

Seminars are normally meant to be small-group sessions where students do most of the work. If students are not sufficiently motivated, however, you could end up teaching them rather than making them responsible for the sessions. The following suggestions may help you to increase your students' motivation levels, which can lead to them getting more out of their seminars.

1. *Explain carefully exactly what seminars are intended to be.* Quite often, things go wrong in seminars because students don't have a clear idea what roles they are expected to take in them. For example, make it clear that the main responsibility for preparing and leading a seminar will go to individual students (or pairs, or groups) in turn, who will then involve the rest of the seminar group in appropriate ways.
2. *Explain* why *seminars are included in the curriculum.* For example, let students know that alongside researching specific aspects of the subject matter, seminars are intended to help them to develop presentation skills which will be invaluable in job interviews in due course. Also remind students of the value of becoming more confident at answering questions 'on one's feet', and how seminars can help to develop this confidence by practice – including trial and error.
3. *Treat seminars seriously yourself.* Students sometimes become demotivated about seminars due to chance remarks along the lines of "Well, it was only a seminar you missed – not a lecture." One way of helping students to appreciate the importance of seminars is to link them firmly to chosen, intended learning outcomes. Remind the whole class that it is through these seminars that their achievement of these outcomes will be developed – and that this achievement will be measured in the normal way through exam questions and coursework assignments, without any further 'teaching' being involved.
4. *Make sure seminars have added value for everyone present.* While it is natural that the individuals or groups who prepare and lead a seminar may derive a great deal of learning pay-off from the experience, it is also important to make sure that the rest of the group derives comparable value. In other words, being present at all the seminars – and participating in them actively – is the

intended learning pathway by which the chosen learning outcomes will be covered.

5 *Plan a series of seminars to be coherent*. Where possible, structure the order of topics covered in a series of seminars in a logical way, so that the overall programme makes sense to the students. This has implications for those students who do the first – and last – seminars, however.

6 *Give students sufficient time to prepare their seminars*. Even though for many students 90 per cent of the preparation is likely to occur in the last 10 per cent of the available time, remind them that their seminars will be much better if they start preparing reasonably early on, so that they can bring second thoughts to bear on their work.

7 *Don't make seminars too long!* It can be more valuable for students to prepare a 10-minute presentation really well, than to prepare a 30-minute presentation rather badly. And if each timetabled seminar session has three or four separate elements in it, at least the attendance is likely to be better. It also helps to bring more variety to the seminars, which allows links to be drawn between different aspects of the subject matter being covered.

8 *Set the groundrules clearly*. For example, negotiate with the whole group about such aspects as:
   - Length of presentation.
   - What sort of handouts may need to be prepared to support the seminar.
   - What sorts of visual aids are expected.
   - How long the question-and-answer session following the presentation will be.
   - Criteria by which the contributions to the seminar series will be assessed.

9 *Consider using peer-assessment for seminars*. This gives students an increased feeling of ownership of the whole process, and encourages them to take seminars more seriously than if they were just being assessed by a lecturer sitting in on the event. It can also encourage those *not* presenting to attend all of the seminars, especially if part of the mark is linked to engaging in the peer-assessment process fairly and equitably.

10 *Don't let particular students suffer inordinately*. For example, when students are particularly shy or nervous leading a seminar can be an ordeal for them. While it is useful to allow all students to be stretched to a reasonable extent by the task of preparing and delivering a seminar, it is also important to ensure that the experience is not too much for any student who could be regarded as having 'special needs' in this particular context. Sometimes, it is wise to arrange an equivalent task for any students who would experience particular discomfort or anxiety in delivering a seminar. For example, when seminars are being delivered by pairs or groups of students, it may be possible to allow roles to be allocated so that anyone who had particular difficulty in the presentation part

of the seminar was involved in preparing the handout or researching the field rather than presenting directly.

Making teaching work in tutorials and workshops

The word 'tutorial' is used to describe a plethora of activities from one-to-one chats between a tutor and a student, through a small gathering of students in a lecturer's office to discuss a particular issue, to groups of 20–25 or even larger timetabled in a classroom after a large lecture. What these formats have in common is that although you may have an agenda for the tutorial, the tutorial should largely be driven by the student agenda. A tutorial may be academic, arranged to discuss a piece of student work or a particular assignment or problems that the student has, or it may be personal. Sometimes a tutorial can be both. You need to be clear about the goals of the tutorial and what the student agenda is. So ask the students what they would like to get out of a tutorial – but be ready to continue to lead them into useful activities if no ready answers are forthcoming from them.

It is important to listen to students as they describe problems and often this is sufficient enough help for students to reach their own solutions. Where you offer advice, check that they have understood. Sometimes it is best to refer students to other sources of information such as written materials, counsellors or other students for help. This is not only a good use of your time but also you may not always be the best person to help. Where this is the outcome, however, always check later that students have found help. It is useful to keep notes of tutorials and to encourage students to do likewise.

Ten ways to motivate students in your tutorials

Tutorials are usually intended to be opportunities for students to deepen their learning, and follow up in more detail the syllabus content which they first encountered in whole-group lectures. However, students often don't quite seem to know how to prepare for tutorials, and can also prove unsure about exactly what they are expected to do during tutorials. The following suggestions may help your students get more from your tutorials.

1 *Work out which aspects of the intended learning outcomes will be directly covered by tutorials.* For example, in maths or science programmes, tutorials are often used to give students the opportunity to practise solving problems or applying theoretical concepts to practical data. It can be useful, when explaining the intended learning outcomes in whole-class contexts, to indicate which aspects of these outcomes will be covered in tutorials.

2 *Don't punish the students who turn up!* Many institutions have problems with student attendance at small-group sessions such as tutorials, sometimes because students don't take them as seriously as lectures. Quite often, this is because students gain the impression from staff that small-group teaching is less important – for example when tutorials are cancelled at short notice by staff. Thus, some students often miss tutorials. It can therefore be frustrating to lecturers when there are students who are late or missing from tutorials, but it is important not to vent this frustration on those students who do turn up. Make it worth their while for having turned up – this is the best way to reverse the trend towards regarding tutorials as missable.
3 *Don't just carry on teaching.* One of the main problems students report about their experience of tutorials is 'it was just a continuation of the lecture'. Sometimes this happens because the students themselves have not identified questions they wish to be answered during tutorials, or because they have not prepared work which it was suggested they do before attending tutorials.
4 *Get to know students' names.* It makes a real difference in small-group contexts such as tutorials if you can call them each by name. When starting a new tutorial series, it can be useful to get students to write their preferred names on sticky labels, and stick these to their clothing. That way, you know what they *prefer* to be called – which may not always be the same as their first name on a class list. This also helps members of the group to get to know each other faster, and this in turn tends to open the group up towards more productive discussions and interactions.
5 *Do appropriate things in small-group tutorials.* Tutorials should maximise the benefits of students being able to interact with each other, and to get to know individual members of staff better. Ideally, each tutorial should be quite different, even when parallel sets of tutorials are following up the same element of subject matter and when there is a set agenda for the tutorials – for example, working though a set of problems to apply to what has been learned in lectures.
6 *Be careful not to advantage particular tutorial groups over others.* Sometimes discussions in a tutorial setting can probe deep into (for example) what standard of exam questions could be expected on a topic. It is important that *other* tutorial groups don't miss out on things relating to the whole class, especially when parallel tutorials are taken by different members of staff. It is best if you note matters such as these which arise in tutorials, and that any advice is saved for a whole-group lecture context so that all the class members can benefit.
7 *Find out what student problems really are.* For example, if you are about to run a small-group tutorial on second order differential equations (or whatever),

give each student a Post-it and ask them all to jot down completions of 'second order differential equations would be much better for me if only ... '. Then ask them to stick the Post-its on a whiteboard, window or wall. You will quickly find out where they are with the topic concerned. It can often be reassuring to students in any case that their problems are shared.

8 *Don't depend too much on students having done prescribed preparation.* One of the most common grumbles shared by tutors is that students turn up not having done the preparation that was briefed in related lectures. Rather than making such students feel really uncomfortable in tutorials (and thereby increasing the risk that they simply don't turn up for future tutorials) it can be better to give *all* the group some time to do short activities in order to set a common baseline from which to move forward during the tutorial. For example, provide a short problem to solve – individually or in sub-groups – or supply one or two article extracts to study for a few minutes before leading into a discussion of matters arising.

9 *Teach by asking questions.* It is useful to fire lots of short, sharp questions randomly during tutorials, so that everyone present becomes accustomed to participating. When the student you ask clearly does not know the answer to a question, however, don't allow discomfort to develop. Ask if anyone else knows the answer to the question – or would like to guess. Alternatively, break the question down into smaller, more-manageable questions, until you reach the level where you start getting answers.

10 *Give students the chance to learn by explaining things.* They don't learn much by letting *you* do all of the explaining. In particular, it can be useful to allow students in twos or threes to explain things to each other, without you taking part – or even trying not to notice, in fact, and only intervening when something is being explained wrongly. The act of explaining things orally (or with the aid of pen and paper, or flipchart, or whiteboard) helps those students who are doing the explaining to deepen their own learning very quickly, and it often helps the rest to hear things being explained by people who have only recently begun to understand what it is they are explaining.

The pressure to teach more students in less time means that seminar and tutorial groups are now often too large to be able to work as one small group. If you attempt to have a discussion in a group of 25, the quieter students tend to be left out. It is probably more productive to address the group as a whole for the first part of the session and then break the group into smaller groups. However, reporting back in plenary can become tiresome so some thought needs to be given to varying this between sessions. Alternatively, you could consider splitting the group in two and scheduling smaller group seminars or tutorials in alternate weeks.

Making small-group learning happen beyond seminars and tutorials

Using small groups to promote interaction within a larger class

To encourage interaction you may wish groups to change regularly. This is relatively easy to achieve, but for it to be successful it is useful to give groups a clear task and a tight deadline. Group interactions of this type may require students to move about the room, so you need to consider the physical layout and whether, and how, groups will efficiently report back to the larger group.

Brainstorming is a useful technique to encourage interaction. It can work well with groups of up to 25 or 30 and can generate a large quantity of ideas without criticism. This can work equally well online. Debates involving students arguing a position can also work well, both in a face-to-face context and also online. Line-ups involve students discussing an issue with other individual students in a group and positioning themselves in a line to represent their relative position on an issue. This can work with groups up to about 25. A jigsaw approach to problem solving involves a topic being divided into subtopics. Small groups work on a particular subtopic, with members becoming knowledgeable in that area. Subsequent groups are reorganised to contain students from each subtopic group who can then pool their knowledge. All these techniques will result in increased interaction between students.

Using small groups for syndicate discussions within a larger class

Small-group discussion can encourage student learning through comparing ideas with each other and allowing students to monitor their own learning independent of their tutors. You will need to consider the advantages of mixing up students or leaving friends or students who have things in common together. It is useful if you are wishing to compare answers from different perspectives in the plenary session to keep cliques together, although students in friendship groups may not be wholly focused on the task. However, if you would like students to explore different perspectives in small groups it is worth mixing students up, although in this case you should obviously allow time for students to introduce themselves.

Crossover groups, where students move between groups drawing on ideas from more than one small group, can work well in stimulating useful discussion. Fishbowl exercises involving a small group discussing an issue whilst a larger group observes and listens can, if not overused, also work well. This technique has applicability for online groupings too.

Using small groups for tutor-student discussion

Some tutors worry about small-group teaching. They worry that students will ask them questions that they can't answer and that it will be difficult to manage a small-group session. Small-group teaching is indeed difficult because you must not only encourage students to think, but you also need a wide knowledge of your subject as well as an appreciation of how groups work. It's important to find out as much as you can about the context before you plan exactly what you're going to do with your small groups. If the session is related to a lecture that someone else is delivering ask if you may sit in on the relevant lecture. Also, try to learn the names of your students. Encourage interaction in tutor-student discussion groups by glancing around the group and drawing in others, thereby discouraging the discussion from drifting into a series of one-to-one dialogues. By glancing around the group you may also pick up non-verbal signals from other students who may like to contribute. You may need to invite reticent members of the group into the discussion, or restrain someone who constantly talks. Sometimes it is useful to pass a question you are asked back to the group to encourage students to formulate their own ideas. In discussions it is helpful to encourage students to share their opinions without you necessarily correcting them. Students may say less if they feel they are being judged and so timing of correction by the tutor is important. It's generally useful not to correct the first contribution a student makes. Some students may find it difficult initially to express their ideas clearly. When this happens quickly check for understanding and clarify the student's position. You can also help to make links between comments, or even better to support students in making connections. You should also redirect the discussion when necessary.

Try to prepare questions prior to the session and encourage students to do the same. Good questioning requires preparation, practice and reflection. Questions serve several purposes in discussion, for example to stimulate students, to test them, to clarify and to make links. It's important when choosing questions to try to put yourself in the students' shoes, to ask some questions directed at higher levels and to be prepared to wait for an answer. Generally it is best if you only prompt groups when they falter – questioning, responding, explaining and summarising for the group. Take care not to dominate the group discussion and balance your role as the expert with that of empathising with students struggling to grasp concepts.

Student-tutor vs student-student small-group work

Small-group, student-tutor learning such as that described above can be expensive in staff time and the recent expansion in student numbers and the increase in class sizes have seen a reduction in the amount of timetabled, tutor led small-group sessions. Tutors have been forced to consider other forms of small-group working, exploiting peer support via students working with other students in teams rather than directly with the tutor expert.

Using teamwork effectively

Teamwork is sometimes regarded as the be all and end all of learning in higher education, particularly at the lower levels. The small-group context can be useful for supporting student participation, independent learning and deep discussion, developing student initiative, self-confidence and key skills, motivating students and promoting student reflection. Student-student interaction can undoubtedly offer something positive to the learning experience. Helping others is a very effective way to learn and interactions between students will in themselves increase achievement. Peer interaction is also useful for stimulating the conflict required for students to grow and develop. In addition, explaining material, issues and concepts to someone else and working with others on a task provide the context for explanation to be given and considered. However, in reality teamwork can be a negative experience for students and many of them hate it. Student-student interaction can contribute to individual learning and the contribution should be capable of adding something that tutors cannot achieve, but there is only value in teamworking if you get it right. Three important factors in creating successful teamwork opportunities are the design of the team task, the design of the context in which the team is working, and whether and how teamwork will be assessed.

Designing the team task

It is worth investing time in the design of team tasks as this will pay dividends in terms of student engagement and the effectiveness of the learning. Firstly, a shared understanding of the task and a consensus of what is involved are very important to the success of a team project. Secondly, it is also important that the task actually requires group participation and thus is not a task that could easily be completed by an individual. Inherently group-based tasks mean that students can't easily split tasks between themselves and are forced to work collaboratively. Undergraduates also tend to perform better on difficult tasks in group contexts than they do individually. Freeloading may be reduced and motivation enhanced by making the task more difficult. If the task is controversial, this can also have the benefit that students within the team are likely to hold incompatible positions and will usually seek more information in order to support their positions.

Setting high-level, controversial tasks without single answers is especially beneficial. It's important that you do not intervene too much, as this will impede team learning around ill-structured problems and interaction around these problems. Finally, think about designing a task that requires a high personal involvement such as reflecting on cultural backgrounds or generating arguments, as students may find these more engaging.

Designing the right context

Groups need to be pulled together and this can be done partially by making group members interdependent. The ideal group working context is when students want the members of their group to succeed rather than need them to succeed. This is more likely to happen in a non-threatening environment. If we ensure that the task is interesting and challenging and that students are prepared with the necessary skills for working in a team then students may find the process of groupwork rewarding. However, it is often the case that groupwork relating to a course needs to be recognised, assessed and rewarded and it is important to hold individuals accountable for their performance and activity within a group. Group members must believe that their contributions to a team project are important if they are investing effort, and their perceptions of others' contributions will also influence their commitment. If individuals believe they are contributing more than others in a group, they will often reduce their efforts to match the other members of the team and avoid being exploited. Sometimes it can be useful if the tutor takes on the role of enforcing discipline, perhaps issuing a yellow or red card and then ultimately expelling from the group those individual students who miss group meetings and so on. This takes the pressure off those students who are contributing to groupwork but who perhaps feel loyalty to peers who are not contributing.

Having student groups compete against one another on a competitive basis can increase motivation of team members to work together but may impact negatively on inter-team relations and specifically on the perceptions that team members have towards other teams. Exchange of ideas within and among groups is more effective and efficient when there is no competition.

Assessing teamwork

Although students seem to work better in groups when not assessed, they seem to prefer to be assessed than not assessed. Traditionally, higher education focuses on the summative assessment of individuals. However, it may be better not to assess students on their individual contributions to a group project but to reward the students as a group, so that they have an incentive to help each other and to encourage each other to perform. To establish what students have learned from small-group teaching it is important that you measure directly the group activity.

Options for assessing teamwork

Assessment of group products	One approach to assessment is via the assessment of group-produced assignments, but students understandably resent freeloaders and it is therefore important to build in safeguards to identify what each student has contributed.
Individual assignments	Another approach is to assess the individual assignments directly derived from groupwork.
Assessment of group behaviour	When assessing group process and behaviour it may be difficult to isolate what exactly to assess. It's not a good idea for you to try to assess interaction. Online discussion groups can be audited but assessment of these, particularly for a large class, can be time-consuming. You may choose to leave assessment to the members of the group, encouraging autonomy and engagement. Be cautious in how you use self-assessment, as students' self-assessment of group contribution tends to be higher than peer or tutor assessments.

Forming functional small groups

Whoever is responsible for forming a group has considerable influence on the success or otherwise of that group. Decisions about the composition, size and group resources can be critical in the early stages. Ideally you could look to train students early on, preferably at the beginning of their course, in how to work in groups but even without training, experience and practice can increase their knowledge of how to behave and their ability to do so appropriately in groups. Try to provide opportunities for the class to mix together and to get to know each other before forming group, as some students may lack the confidence to get to know others in a group.

There are several approaches to forming groups, all with their own pros and cons. Suppose you've got a larger group of students (20 upwards) and you want to get them into groups of four or five. There are quite a few ways to do this, and once again all with their own pros and cons.

- *Let them form their own sub-groups.* These are sometimes called 'friendship' groups because of the likelihood of friends already being close to each other, or may be 'geographical' groups chosen on the basis of where people are in the room when the groups are forming. One advantage is that students who like each other or know each other may work well together. A clear disadvantage here is that there will often end up being a 'reject group', based on those students who didn't get into a friendship group quickly, and such students may start the groupwork on a more depressed note.
- *Alphabetical groups.* Class lists are one way of predetermining the composition of groups. In one way it's the forming of random groups, but if the same technique is being used by several tutors the group composition may be boringly similar in different subjects.
- *Really random groups.* You could go round the larger group, calling out "A, B, C, D, E ... " and giving each student a letter, then ask "all the 'As' collect in this corner, all the 'Bs' over there ... " and so on. One advantage is that students may get to work with a range of other students. The disadvantage is that truly random groupings could result in some undesirable problems between students.
- *Successively different groups.* One way of making this happen is to use sticky labels on which you've already written a three-digit code and onto which students can write their preferred names to use as name badges. The code could consist of:

  A symbol (triangle, asterisk, square, or sticky coloured dots).
  A letter (A, B, C, etc).
  A number (1, 2, 3, etc).

  The first group membership could be "All the people with the same symbol collect together ... ", then the second group task could be "Please go into groups by letter – the 'As' over here, the 'Bs' there ... " and so on; and finally the third group arrangement could be "All the '1s' here please, the '2s' there", and so on. That way everyone will be in an entirely different group three times over, and students will interact successively with a wide range of the overall number of people in the whole room.
- *Engineered groups.* This is often the most successful way to form groups, allowing the tutor to select groups based on specific criteria.

The top ten factors to consider when forming small groups

1 *Size.* Group size can affect interaction and group intimacy and is an important factor. When deciding upon group size you should consider what the group will be doing; why the students are working together in a group; whether you

will be leading the group or if it is to be a student group; how long the group will be working together; whether you intend to split the group into subgroups; and whether the group will still be large enough if one or two members leave the group. The larger the group, the greater the pool of resources available for solving problems. As group size increases, however, members have fewer opportunities to participate and less ownership so that there is a danger that one or two members will begin to dominate the group whilst some students may not contribute at all. Smaller groups may foster closer relationships and higher individual participation and there is more chance of the group sharing leadership than in a larger group. Most practitioners agree that five to seven members is generally the optimum size for student groups. This also applies to online groups because students are more self-conscious if they know they are interacting with 100 students than a much smaller group of students. Small-group size can be a major factor in the success of higher education computer conferencing, but equally it is important that group size is not too small as a certain amount of activity is required for successful online conferencing. In the case of tutor led groups a group size of up to 12 can work well, although with very small tutor led groups you need to be careful not to dominate. Brainstorming can benefit from larger groups.

2 *Composition.* Individual students will contribute differently depending on which other students are in the group. A powerful influence on individual performance within a group is the personal friendships or dislikes of fellow members and this shouldn't be underestimated. When allocating students to groups you need to consider what kind of activities the group will be engaged in, friendship groups, and how well particular students have worked together in the past. It is worth considering mixing students of different abilities when groups have to solve problems, as a teaching process between the students can take place which benefits all.

3 *Ability.* Group ability composition can affect student learning within the group. Low ability students can gain most from being placed in mixed ability groups because of the individual assistance that low ability students receive from their more able peers. The more able students also benefit from explaining and therefore by gaining a deeper understanding. Medium ability students, however, can gain most when put into groups with similarly able students, learning through sharing in the giving and receiving of support and explanation and forming high group cohesiveness. Same ability groupings support group cohesiveness but do not provide as good an environment for conflict or for opportunities for learning through explanation to other students. However, mixed ability groups are generally better for productive interaction, for the achievement of goals and for group decision making.

4 *Cohesion.* It is often better if members of a group know each other prior to

group formation because the emotional needs and undercurrents can be more powerful than the intellectual aspects of a group. The sense of social belonging and identity that students can get from being a member of a group should not be underestimated as it is essential for higher learning, positive self-evaluation, productive interaction and task performance. Some advocate the usefulness of inter-group competitions to build up group cohesion but these have to be carefully considered.

5 *Participation*. In a group it is quite common to find one or two students dominating the discussion and activity, with other group members not participating. Clearly this can be a problem although it is not necessarily the case that non-participating students are not learning. However, fairly equal participation is clearly the ideal and you may need to consider how you will monitor or possibly assess participation to encourage this. In organising seating for small-group learning, nervous students can be encouraged to participate if they are sitting opposite a sympathetic tutor or sympathetic student peer. A dominating student can be quietened by being seated next to the tutor. It may be worth considering the introduction of procedures to deal with participation issues.

6 *Procedures*. Procedures may be necessary to ensure the smooth running of the group and the achievement of aims. It may be prudent for you to specify procedures for small groups or to leave it to each group to decide on any procedures relating to how the group will decide on agendas, make decisions, ensure the full involvement of each member and monitor and evaluate progress.

7 *Structure*. You could choose to distribute a set of roles to the group or leave this up to the group to decide, as the structure of the group may change according to the nature of the activity. In tutorless groups, the leadership role may move around different members of the group.

8 *Aims*. Successful groups often have both social and task-related aims. Social aims include developing a sense of belonging and group loyalty and the ability to work cooperatively and should complement the task aims. If the social aims are not present, students may have no sense of commitment to the group. If the task aims are missing they may feel they are not achieving anything worthwhile. Additionally group members are likely to have their own personal aims and these may have little to do with the aims of the group. Sometimes these personal aims may undermine the intended aims of the group. It's important for success to be clear about what all the aims of the group are and it is useful if you can encourage students to be open about their aims with the group.

9 *Task*. Often not enough attention is given to specifying groupwork activities. It is important that the task is actually a group task and not one that could

just as easily (or more easily) be carried out by an individual student. You should invest effort in specifying the task.

10 *Physical environment.* You should ensure that where groups are meeting the surroundings are conducive to groupwork. The location of a group meeting can be quite important. The lecturer's room underlines the lecturer's authority, whereas a table in the refectory has no privacy and can be too noisy to allow effective groupwork. Apart from their usefulness as a writing surface, tables create a physical barrier which may be reassuring, although if there are no tables this can encourage openness. The further apart students are, the less interaction there is likely to be. Dominant students will tend to choose seats in the centre of a group and shy students may sit outside the group. It is useful to consider whether it is possible to move furniture to facilitate eye contact and to improve communication.

Nine ways to help your students to get the most out of small-group sessions

1 *Help your students to become ready for assessment.* This is the sharp end of tutoring, not least because most forms of assessment involve winners and losers – and it is very uncomfortable to be a loser. Perhaps the most important attribute of an excellent tutor is the ability to make students feel the tutor is 'on their side' in the assessment battle. Even when tutors are going to be doing the assessment themselves, it is really helpful for students to feel that everything possible is being done by their tutors to maximise their chances of succeeding at the assessment hurdle. Preparing for assessment should not degenerate into a 'Guess What's in the Tutor's Mind' game – there should be no guesswork involved, and students should have a clear idea of what's in their tutors' minds. In particular, it helps when tutors strive to help students to make sense of what they have learned, so that they feel they have 'digested' the information involved and turned it into their own knowledge, and have a sense of ownership of their achievement well before the time when they are required to demonstrate evidence of their achievement of the learning outcomes.

2 *Negotiate agreements with your small-group students.* The main advantage of learning agreements is that they help students to take ownership of the need to learn, and that because it is an *agreement* they feel they have played a part in working out the timescales involved, and deciding *what* to learn, *how best* to go about learning it, and *at what level* the learning needs to take place. The best ways of making it *feel* like an agreement to students is to ensure that they see that their tutors have their own parts to play in bringing the agreement to fruition.

3 *Help students to make sense of their targets*. In particular, clarify exactly what is meant by the intended learning outcomes. The problem with such outcomes is that they are often written in a foreign language to students – 'academese'! It is all very well to use phrases such as 'demonstrate your understanding of … ' but students need to know exactly *how* they are expected to do this in due course. They need to know what the *evidence* will look like when they have 'understood' something to the level required. They need to know what the standards are that will be applied to this evidence. They need to understand the contexts in which this evidence will be generated – whether it is exams, coursework, practical work, independent work and so on. Small-group contexts are ideal for helping your students to find out exactly what the intended learning outcomes mean in practice.

4 *Help students to see the importance of becoming better at learning.* Study skills are important, not just in the context of helping students work their way towards succeeding in their present studies, but for life in general. Students will continue to need to learn new things far beyond those years when they are involved in formal study, and the better they become at being able to take on new learning targets and to work systematically and purposefully towards achieving these targets, the better the quality of their future lives will be. Even when an element of learning has proved unsuccessful, there are usually useful study skills lessons to be gained from the experience. Study skills cannot be directly 'taught' – they are (like just about everything else) learned by doing, practice, trial and error, and experience. Tutors can use small-group learning contexts to help by setting up practice opportunities, responding to the trial and error, and helping students to learn productively from each others' experience.

5 *Help students to manage their time.* Time-management is not only an essential study skill – it is a life skill. Probably the most important single element of time-management is 'getting started' on each task – if something isn't started it will never get finished! Therefore, tutors in small-group contexts can help students to get their learning underway by pointing out that human nature tries to find 'work avoidance tactics' which delay getting started, but that once recognised as such it is perfectly possible to counteract them. A task that has only been started for five minutes is much more likely to become completed than a task which has not yet been started. Therefore, tutors can help by making sure that tasks get started in face-to-face contact time, even if only for those vital minutes which will allow students to go away and continue them in their own time and at their own speed.

6 *Help students to balance their act.* An important addition to good time-management is good *task-management.* In other words, help students to prioritise their tasks. This involves making sure that the important ones get done, and the less

important ones aren't given too much time. Tutors can help students in working out what exactly are the most important tasks, and putting these at the top of the agenda. Tutors can also help by advising on sensible limits for the important tasks, so that they don't just swallow up all of students' available time and energy, and leave other important tasks un-started. It can be better to do an hour's worth on each of three tasks than to spend all three hours on one task, especially if all three tasks contribute to the assessment agenda.

7 *Help students to identify questions, and seek the answers to these questions.* "If I knew what the exam questions were going to be, I could easily prepare for the exam" many students say. But they *can* know what the questions are going to be. "Any important piece of information can simply be regarded as the answer to a question" is a useful way of helping students to think in terms of questions rather than information. Once they know what a question is, they can find out the answer in any of the following ways:

- Look it up in a book or handout.
- Look it up on the internet.
- Ask other students and see if they know the answer.
- Ask other people altogether.
- Ask an expert witness – for example, you.

Encourage students to make question banks of their own. In other words, get them to jot down all the questions which they might need some day to be able to answer, to demonstrate their learning. It is really useful to start with the intended learning outcomes, and turn these into long lists of very short, sharp questions, so that students get the message that if they can answer lots of straightforward questions, they can in fact answer much more complex questions, as these just amount to a collection of the shorter ones in practice.

It can be particularly useful to get students to make question banks in small groups, so that the range of questions is better, and to help them to learn from each other's questions. Tutors can give valuable responses regarding which questions are the really important ones, to help to steer students to the main agendas of their learning.

8 *Help students to become better readers.* Not all students come from households where walls are lined with bookshelves. Not all students devour books. Indeed, for many students, reading is not a particularly pleasurable activity, unless they are reading about something about which they are already passionate. Tutors can help students to realise that they don't have to devour books, but that all that may be needed is to *use* them successfully to find information from them. In other words, *information retrieval* (whether from books or websites) does not necessarily mean reading everything in sight, but homing in to what's important. This goes back to starting reading with *questions* in mind. If

students read a page of text pre-armed with five questions, they are much more likely to get what is intended out of the page than if they just 'read' it.

Help students to make good use of headings, sub-headings, contents pages, and the indexes of books and articles. Help them to read in 'search and retrieve' mode, so they are looking for particular things, and noting them down as they find them, rather than simply reading page after page vainly hoping that some of the information there will 'stick'.

9 *Help students get their revision act together.* Most students regard revision for tests or exams as a bore! This is all too often because they have previously tackled the job in boring ways. They have tried to 'learn' their subject materials in non-productive ways, and become disillusioned. A good start is for tutors to reinforce that revision is simply about systematically becoming better able to answer questions – that's what exams and tests actually measure. As with anything else, the best way to become better at something is to do it – and do it again – until it becomes second nature. Students who have practised answering a question seven times in a fortnight are very likely indeed to get it right the eighth time – in the test.

Another way tutors can help students regarding revision is by alerting them to what *not* to revise. There's no point spending a lot of time and energy on learning something that won't or can't be the basis of a sensible exam or test question. Similarly, anything that *isn't* directly related to an intended learning outcome will not be on the revision agenda – if it were important it would have been there among those intended outcomes.

Tutors can remind students that what is measured by tests and exams isn't what's in their heads – it's usually what comes out of their pens or pencils. In other words, it's their evidence of achievement of the intended learning outcomes that is the basis for assessment, and the best revision processes involve purposeful practice at evidencing that achievement.

Checklist: preparing your small-group session

Question	Yes	Not yet	Not applicable	Action planning
Do I know how many small-group sessions I will be running with this class?				
Do I know whether I'll be taking all of the class in separate repeated sessions, or whether other colleagues will be running parallel small-group sessions alongside mine?				

Question	**Yes**	**Not yet**	**Not applicable**	**Action planning**
Do I know whether the small-group sessions will be tutorials (in other words, led by me) or seminars (where I'll get students to prepare and lead elements), or a mixture of both?				
Do I know whether I will be running associated lectures with the students, or whether the lectures will be given by other colleagues?				
Have I worked out the intended learning outcomes for these students, in language I can share with the students?				
Do I know where these small-group sessions fit in to the overall course or module my students are studying?				
Do I know whether I'll be using the same teaching room for all of these sessions with these students?				
Have I prepared task-briefings for the work students will do before the sessions?				
Have I prepared task-briefings for a range of possible tasks students could do during the sessions?				
Have I prepared handout materials, slides or overheads to accompany these sessions?				
Do I know whether any equipment I may need in these sessions is available in the rooms concerned?				

Review checklist: after running a small-group session

Question	Very well	Quite well	Not well	Action planning
Did I introduce and explain the intended learning outcomes clearly to the students?				
Did the session work well in terms of these outcomes – did most of the students achieve the outcomes?				
Did the activities I planned for the students work out well in practice?				
Did I manage to involve *all* of the students in doing things during the session?				
For seminar-type sessions, did I manage to let students themselves play a full part in delivering their contributions?				
Did I succeed in getting the students to work together in different combinations, so that they made the most of collaborative working?				
Did I manage not to intervene too readily if the session 'got stuck' temporarily?				
How well was I able to use the small-group session to address questions and problems raised by individual students?				
Did I bring the session to a rounded and punctual close?				
What was the best thing about this particular small-group session?				
What was the least satisfactory thing about this particular small-group session?				
What is the single most important thing I will do differently the next time I run a similar session?				

Solving common problems in small-group teaching

How students sometimes spoil small-group work

It is useful to think about some of the things which can get in the way of small-group teaching. Later in this section, we'll return to some of these in "What can I do when … ?" mode, but for now let's just list some of the potential problems, starting with some difficulties which students can cause us.

1 *Students don't take it seriously*. Students often seem to regard lectures as much more important than seminars or tutorials. This is sometimes our fault – if *we* don't seem to be taking small-group teaching as seriously as lectures, students are quick to pick up the vibes.
2 *Some students don't turn up*. This follows on from the problem above, but it makes our job all the more difficult if we don't know till the last minute what size group we are likely to be working with.
3 *Some students come unprepared*. They turn up without having done the pre-reading or preparatory work which we set in advance of the small-group sessions.
4 *Some students tend to dominate*. It can be tiresome for their group-mates, and we often need to change group membership regularly so that the dominating students are spread around.
5 *Some students are 'passengers'*. In large-group teaching, we can't always get everyone to participate actively (though we can try), and 'passengers' can usually get away with not contributing. In small-group contexts, however, 'passenger' behaviours become more noticeable, and we need to try all the harder to make sure that small-group learning is active for all those present.
6 *Students may fall out with each other!* Conflict can arise in small-group contexts, particularly when student contributions to the products of the work of a group are assessed, and when contributions have been uneven.

How we can spoil small-group work!

The things which do go wrong are not all down to students. The following short list shows that our own actions can lead to small-group work being unproductive.

1 *Tutors sometimes carry on teaching, rather than keeping students working actively*. Particularly if the students don't engage actively, or ask questions, it's all too easy just to keep the small-group session going by expanding on what we may have covered in lectures.

2 *Tutors sometimes make students feel uncomfortable.* For example, when students turn up but have not done the expected preparation for a small-group session, it is natural enough to exhort them to greater efforts in future. However, if they respond badly to such pressure, they will become more likely simply to skip a future session if they haven't prepared for it.
3 *Tutors sometimes allow the domineering, and fail to bring in the shy violets.* We need to find ways of equalising contributions in small-groups, such as using Post-its to get everyone to contribute ideas before opening up the floor for discussion.
4 *Tutors sometimes fail to make it clear what each small-group session is intended to achieve.* It is useful to continue the practice used for lectures regarding the specifying of some precise, intended learning outcomes for small-group sessions.
5 *Some groups can become 'disadvantaged'.* For example, if a particular group gets into detailed discussion of what the assessment standards are, or what would be reasonable exam questions to expect, other groups which did not have this discussion are disadvantaged. Ideally, it is best to have any discussion about standards in the whole-group session.

In the discussion below, we look at some of the most frequently-asked questions we get when running workshops about small-group teaching, and offer a few suggestions about tactics which can be used to address each problem in turn.

What can I do when students don't turn up for my small-group sessions?

In practice, there's little mileage in trying to 'force' students to turn up to any element in their programmes, and when students don't regard small-group teaching as particularly important, the problem of absenteeism increases. However, a combination of one or more of the following tactics can improve things sometimes ...

- *Make sure it's worth turning up for.* When the students who *are* present come away with something they would not have wanted to miss (be it handouts, the light dawning, tasks they found valuable doing, and so on), word can get around and attendance can improve.
- *Ask some regular absentees "What's wrong?".* Sometimes there could be a timetable clash you didn't know about, or travel difficulties relating to a particular time slot. Sometimes, of course, the answer can be "I didn't find the sessions helpful", and we may need to probe gently into "Why not exactly?" and remain ready to listen to the responses.

- *Keep the assessment agenda on the table.* When students can see that each small-group session has a bearing on helping them become ready for future exam questions, or can help them to see what's being looked for in coursework assignments, students are less likely to be absent.
- *Include at least* some *coursework mark for 'participation'.* Don't just include it for *attendance* however, or the odd student may come along but not join in!

What can I do when students refuse to do a task?

This is an awkward one. If *all* the students won't start your task, it's worse. The following tactics can help ...

- *Make sure the task briefing is really clear.* Explain again exactly what you want them to do. It can be useful to say "What it really means is ... " and to then put it into straightforward language.
- *Show the task on a slide or overhead, or give it out as a handout.* Sometimes, students can get the gist of a task rather better if they can see it and hear it at the same time.
- *Try to find the block.* For example, ask students "Which part of the task are you having problems with?" and see if clarifying that part helps them to get started.
- *Break the task into smaller bits.* Ask students just to do the first bit now, and then explain the later stages one by one when they're properly under way.
- *Ask them to work in pairs to start with.* You can then go round any pairs who still seem reluctant to start the task, and find out more about what it is that is stopping them.
- *Set a precise deadline for the first part of the task.* Sometimes this is enough to get them started.
- *Resist the temptation to keep talking.* Give them some time when there's really nothing more to come, and it's clear that you expect them to get stuck into the task. A few seconds of solemn silence may seem interminable to you, but the resistance to getting started with the task may be fading away.

What can I do when students don't get on with each other?

This is more likely to happen in small groups than large groups. The following tactics can help ...

- *Re-arrange group membership now and then.* This can be done randomly, but check that particular pairs of students who don't seem to be getting on are now moved apart into different groups.

- *Give them all a task to start on their own.* Sometimes if all of the students have already invested some energy in thinking through the topic before the actual group work begins, differences between students are pushed further into the background.
- *Make the first part an individual written task.* For example, give out Post-its, and ask everyone to jot down a single idea relevant to the task. Then when everyone is armed with at least one idea, the chances of students not getting on with each can be reduced.
- *Go closer to the people who don't seem to be getting on.* Sometimes, your proximity will cause them to bury any differences – for the moment at least. You may also then get the chance to work out what exactly has been causing the confrontation between the students concerned.
- *Watch out for the occasional 'difficult student'.* When the same person doesn't get on in groupwork contexts with different individuals, it can be worth having a quiet word. Just sometimes, you'll find the odd student who really doesn't function well in group contexts.

What can I do when one student dominates the group?

This is a frequent occurrence. Sometimes the causes are innocent enough – enthusiasm, knowing a lot about the topic, and so on. One or more of the following tactics may help you to balance things out ...

- *Set appropriate ground rules at the start of small-group work.* It can be useful to say a little about leadership and followership – making the point that in many small-group situations in real life, too many leaders can mitigate against success, and that everyone needs to be able to be a good follower for at least some of the time.
- *Re-arrange group membership regularly.* This means that the domineering student moves on, and doesn't dominate other students for too long.
- *Intervene gently.* For example, after the domineering student comes to a pause ask "Would someone else now like to add to this please?"
- *Have a quiet word.* Do this with the domineering student outside the group context, for example by giving suggestions about 'air time' and allowing everyone's views to be heard.
- *Change the dynamic.* Appoint the domineering student as chairperson for a particular activity, with the brief not to make any input on that task, but to coordinate everyone else's thinking.
- *Don't fight it too hard.* Recognise that domineering is a common human trait, and that domineering people often reach distinguished positions in the world around us and thus may be developing relevant skills in small-group contexts.

Conclusion

There are many potential pitfalls when working with small groups. Often the difficulties of managing dysfunctional groups in terms of staff time, plus students' own problems with groupwork, can lead to an unsatisfactory experience for all. However, this chapter has tried to present guidelines for effective and efficient small-group learning which are equally applicable to face-to-face and online group working contexts. Of primary importance when setting group tasks is to choose tasks that are genuinely group-based, challenging and engaging and to ensure that groups are interdependent. When forming groups consider carefully the mechanism you will use and if possible give small groups time to become familiar with one another. Lay out any ground rules and then be prepared to step back. Your role will often be that of a facilitator of group learning rather than an instructor.

5

Working with large groups

This chapter addresses the following questions:

- What are we trying to achieve when working with large groups?
- How can we engage students in large-group learning?
- How can we effectively integrate and use feedback in large groups?
- How can we contingency plan for large-group lectures?

What are we trying to achieve?

The large-group lecture remains a standard on most courses although its role has changed over the last decade.

As is evidenced by low attendance at many lectures, the emergence of the internet and information on demand has reduced the importance of the lecture as a primary means of conveying information. Whilst lectures can continue to provide a useful role in providing an overview and in knitting together the different threads of a course, this can only happen if students see value enough in the lectures to attend. It is timely, therefore, for us to address many of the shortcomings of the traditional lecture, and to recognise the potential that now exists to move away from syllabus dissemination to focus on addressing a concept fully, as well as trying to inspire students.

Your goal when working with large groups, as in any other learning context, is to support student learning. Working with a large group, however, presents particular challenges as natural interaction and discussion can be restricted and opportunities for formative feedback and addressing learner needs must be carefully planned.

Whilst it is useful to discuss the best ways to plan and design a lecture and how to develop lecture resources, it is important that you don't lose sight of what you are trying to achieve in a lecture. The critical success factor of any lecture will always be student engagement and whilst it is helpful to give a professional and credible impression, the lecturer's flexibility to address student needs in a large-group lecture will always be more important. We also would do well to remember that there is little point to delivering a lecture that is forgotten. You need to adopt an approach to lecture design and delivery that impacts upon diverse student learning in a lasting way.

It is good practice to identify what it is you are hoping students will learn from a lecture, and to explain to your students what they should be getting out of the lecture. To start a lecture well, it is helpful to be able to say to the students "By the end of this lecture, you'll be able to … " and then to list three of four things students should be able to do by the end of that particular lecture as a direct result of being there. It is equally useful to return to the intended learning outcomes in the last few minutes of the lecture and to ask students how well they now feel that they have achieved the outcomes, possibly asking them to show for each outcome in turn whether they feel they have 'completely achieved', 'partly achieved' or 'not yet achieved' it by a show of raised hands – two, one, and none respectively. This not only reminds the students of what they should now be able to do, but also lets you know how well your lecture worked.

Hint: ***if you're using PowerPoint, make your very last slide one that repeats the intended learning outcomes. You can get to that last slide instantly simply by entering '99' (or any number greater or equal to that of the number of that last slide) at the keyboard and pressing 'Enter'. This means that even if you haven't managed to get through all of the slides in your presentation, you can seamlessly go to that rounding-up slide.***

Whilst the large-group lecture brings with it the biggest challenges of any learning forum, if we get it right it also offers the greatest opportunity for efficient teaching and learning. So how do we ensure we are engaging students in large-group lectures?

How can we engage students in large-group learning?

Traditionally many lectures were quite passive affairs, with lecturers disseminating content in a rather linear manner to students who were expected to listen, take notes and keep quiet. However, it is no longer necessary to rely on the lecture to disseminate large amounts of content, and given the range of learning styles and cultures represented in many lecture theatres today the traditional lecture format may fail to meet the needs of students. In a world of soundbites and multimedia, an increasing proportion of today's students do not have highly developed listening skills and the increasing diversity of the student population and the rising expectations of students used to processing multiple messages and multiple media simultaneously mean that we need to rethink the large-group lecture.

Non-engagement

Non-attendance, lateness and talking in lectures may all indicate a lack of engagement. Sometimes there may be quite legitimate reasons for apparent non-engagement, but students may also be getting bored – or tired – or may be trying to catch up with someone else's assignment deadline. Basically, students are more likely to attend a session if they:

- are able to be there;
- want to be there;
- need to be there.

And equally, students are more likely to engage in large-group learning if they:

- are able to engage;
- want to engage;
- need to engage.

The following ten-point plan is a good way of minimising disruption in lectures and of ensuring that conditions are conducive to student engagement:

1. *Agree some ground rules with the whole group in the first session*. For example, if quite a lot of the students have to come from another session at the other end of the campus, negotiate to start promptly five minutes *after* the normal time.
2. *Link each and every lecture firmly to the assessment agenda*. Students don't like to miss out on (for example) clarification of what a typical exam question could reasonably ask of them. Give students cues and clues about how this particular lecture 'counts' in due course. Whenever you say "You'll need today's material for exam questions like (so-and-so)", you'll notice students jotting something down!
3. *Keep yourself tuned into WIIFM*. ('What's In It For Me?') – a perfectly intelligent question for any student to have in mind. Always make time to remind students about *why* a topic is included, and *how* it will help them in due course. Try to add value. Make sure that the students who do turn up feel that it has been well worth doing so. Give them a useful and enjoyable learning experience.
4. *Consider the value of starting each lecture with a bang* – something the students will be keen not to miss, for example a different assessment hint every session.
5. *Don't wait for late students*. Those who came punctually deserve to be getting some value, so get started even if the audience is sparse.

6 *Give students something to talk about with near neighbours sometime in a lecture.* In other words, *legitimise* their talking for a few minutes, and let them get the need to talk out of their system.
7 *Don't necessarily assume students are being rude.* Sometimes, one will have asked another to explain or repeat something that has been missed. Sometimes they could be translating what you say into another language for each other. Often students can't avoid arriving late.
8 *If an interruption is noisy don't just carry on trying to ignore it.* That often makes the problem get worse. Pause, looking at the people who are making the noise until they stop – or until the other students shut them up for you.
9 *Resist the temptation to be sarcastic.* If students get a rough ride from you, they may decide not to come to the next lecture.
10 *Don't ask an 'offender' to leave!* If they actually *refuse* to leave, you'll have a much more difficult problem to deal with. Never issue a threat that you would not in practice be able to implement.

Delivery

For the teacher's part the focus when working with large groups should be on explaining concepts in the clearest possible way and trying to establish a rapport with your students.

Establishing a rapport

It can be quite challenging to establish a rapport with a large group where eye contact is difficult and where there is considerable geographical distance between lecturer and students. Many lecture theatres are now equipped with microphones, lecterns and complex control panels which control everything from the theatre lighting to a 'fresh air boost'. Whilst these tools can be used effectively to deliver a professional presentation, they offer little to support a comfortable dialogue between learner and teacher.

However, large-group lectures present us with a fairly unique opportunity. Mass events, by their nature, may be highly charged and being part of a large crowd can be quite uplifting, particularly where the crowd's shared experience is memorable or emotional. Learning can be most effective when we engage students on an emotional level and it is worth considering how we might exploit the lecture theatre. For example, it now takes little effort to use music in a lecture theatre. There is evidence that music can not only lift our mood (it's possible to measure emotional response to music with a heart-rate monitor) but that there is also a link between music and cognition (Dribben, 2006; Lamont, 2005). If we are hoping to engage the emotions of learners then music is an excellent tool.

Another useful tool available to the lecturer delivering to a large group is the story. Anecdotes that are relevant to the students' experience or that bring a concept to life can work very well in a lecture theatre, particularly where they are supported by visual or other stimuli. It is just as easy to tell a story to 200 as it is to an individual and just as effective. Stories can be quite easy to absorb and recall and because students may relax when they are listening to a story they are a useful way of building a rapport with a large group.

Another approach you may consider is 'team' teaching. Delivering a session as part of a team, or even with just one other colleague, can open up a whole range of possibilities for debate and the presentation of different perspectives. If students see that their lecturer's perspective is simply that – one person's view – they are perhaps more likely to think critically about the issues raised in lectures. It also takes the pressure off you, particularly if you are delivering with a colleague you trust to flag up things you've missed.

To be effective you should try to make lectures enjoyable. Although you have to be careful with humour, if you are able to introduce an appropriately funny slide, or an amusing anecdote, or a play on words, these can work wonders at restoring students' concentration levels. Then follow up something funny with an important point, while you've still got their full attention.

Finally, it's useful if you can cause the students to *like* you. Smile. Be human. Look at them. Respond to them. If they like you, they're more likely to come to your *next* lecture too.

Explaining clearly to a large group

When delivering to a large group, the design of the support materials is particularly important and you should consider using a range of approaches and materials. Well-designed materials can go a long way to clarifying explanations, aiding post-lecture recall and supporting interaction between teacher and students, and the modern lecture theatre allows us to exploit a wide range of resources with relatively little effort. Most importantly, lecturers should be seen and heard. Use a mike if it helps. Don't just say "Can you hear me at the back?" – ask someone in the back row a question and find out. And don't dim the lights to show your slides at the expense of students no longer being able to see *you.*

Visual aids

The design of visual aids can contribute significantly to clear explanation in a large lecture. Most lecturers use slides or overheads. Slides are a useful comfort blanket for us as lecturers. A well-produced set of slides gives an immediate impression of a professional and credible lecture. Slides allow your students to *see* things on the screen at the same time as they *hear* about them from you, and this means a better chance of your students making sense there and then of the topic in hand. However, it can get quite boring for learners if *all* the slides are just print and lists of bullet points. Slides can, with a little effort, be quite sophisticated – containing all sorts of visual information. It takes very little knowledge or time to import photographs, diagrams, or snippets of film into slides and this presents a great opportunity to enrich the lecture.

Navigation Hint: ***slides can allow you to make your lecture more flexible and allow you to respond to what actually happens in the session. If using PowerPoint slides, prepare a paper handout for yourself containing all of the slides, say six per page. Write clearly the numbers of the slides on your paper copies. When giving your presentation, you can go to any slide at any time, and in any order, simply by keying in '5' then 'Enter' to go to slide 5, '23' for slide 23, and so on. This is particularly useful when students ask a question and you may want to go back to an earlier slide, or for when time is running out and you want to skip ahead to a later slide, and so on. It gives you full control of which slides you show when, without having to clumsily run backwards or forwards through slides you're not actually going to use on that occasion. Remember, however, to tick off on your paper copy which slides you did in fact use (or not use) so that later on you still have a record of exactly what you covered in that particular lecture.***

Ten tips for good slides

1. *Don't put too much on any slide.* A few questions, headlines or bullet points are better than solid paragraphs. Detailed information is best left for handout materials.
2. *Use large fonts, to ensure that everything can be read from the back of the room.* Check this out – or get a colleague to run quickly through your slides with you yourself sitting at the back.
3. *Check which colours work well.* Some text colours (notably orange and red) don't come across clearly at the back of the room. The software allows you to have dark text against light backgrounds and vice-versa. However, light text against dark backgrounds works rather badly if you can't dim the lighting in the lecture room (for example, if there are windows without good blinds).
4. *Try to fill only the top half or two-thirds of any slide.* Students may have to peer around each other's heads to see anything right at the bottom of a slide – you can tell this by when they move their heads as you reveal a 'last bullet point' on a slide.

5 *Use pictures, cartoons, and graphs.* They help to bring your subject to life.
6 *Don't include detailed graphs, tables or flowcharts.* If the detail will not be clearly visible at the back of the room it is better included in handout materials than on-screen in the lecture room.
7 *Don't include 'slide numbers' on slides:* (The software allows automatic numbering if that's what you want.) Not including slide numbers gives you the freedom to pick-and-mix your slides, without your students realising that you're skipping some of them!
8 *Don't issue 3-per-page or 6-per-page handout copies of your slides in advance.* This robs you of opportunities to 'surprise' your students with unexpected quotations, or even 'fun' slides. In addition, if you're going to pick-and-mix from your slides as in the 'hint' above, remember to issue later only those slides you did actually use.
9 *Don't cause 'death by bullet point'.* It gets mighty tedious for students if successive bullet points always come one at a time in the same exactly predictable way. Make different slides *look* different – include some charts or pictures, where possible. If you're confident with technology put in some optional, very short video clips now and then – but nothing vital (which would matter if it didn't work straightaway).
10 *Learn from other people's use of slides.* Whenever possible sit in on colleagues' lectures and conference presentations and see what works well for others – and what doesn't.

Hint: *don't keep slides up for too long because students will keep gazing at the screen. Get them to look at you now and then. There are few things worse than a slide staying up too long after it has been used – for example when you've moved on to talk about something else, or are answering a question from your audience – and it then just becomes a distraction for your students. An easy way of switching your slides off when using PowerPoint is to press 'B' on the keyboard – 'B' for black. When you want your slide back, all you need to do is press 'B' again – 'B' for back. This is far safer than risking switching off the data projector – some machines can take minutes to warm up again.*

A particularly useful feature of slides is that usually you can see your slides on a computer screen (or on the OHP) in front of you, without turning round to the main screen onto which the image is projected, which means you can talk about your slides without turning your back on the students. The convenience of slides has led to their ubiquity. However, it's important to remember that slides do not in themselves constitute a lecture, they are simply aids. Consider giving a lecture without PowerPoint, or at a basic level think about incorporating other types of simple aid such as the basic flipchart or whiteboard.

Handouts

Students like handouts and expect handouts.

The trouble, however, with handouts is that your students can switch off mentally during your lectures if they feel that all of the information is to be found in their handouts. When students coming out of lectures are asked "Tell me what the lecture was about?", they will admit "Sorry, I don't know– I've got the handout, but I haven't read it properly yet!"

If you have a handout it is important to make sure that students take away from the lecture quite a lot more than just the information in it. Good ideas on using handouts are:

- Making handout materials interactive so that students do things with the handout during the lecture, and come out with something to which they have added a lot of their own ideas and thoughts, thus adding value to it.
- Designing handouts to support student note making rather than note taking. For example, now and then during your lecture, give them a couple of minutes to make a summary on the handout of what you've been talking about. It can then be useful to ask them to compare their summaries with students sitting close to them, and to add to their own any interesting or important points that they may have missed
- Making handout materials complementary to the lecture. Explain to your students that "Aspects we are not going to talk about today are included in your handout" and use the lecture to focus on key aspects rather than on disseminating the whole syllabus content.

Hint: ***it can be useful to have handouts with blank boxes for students to write into during lectures. In other words, have spaces for them to do tasks at a few points in your lecture. Rather than actually print the task briefings on the handout materials, it works better simply to put 'Task 1', 'Task 2' and so on in the empty boxes. This helps to stop students getting ahead of where you want them to be, but more usefully it gives you the chance to adjust the actual tasks depending on how the class seems to be getting on with the subject, and depending on the amount of time you find you have available. It is useful to have slides***

or overheads ready of a few alternative tasks, so that you can decide exactly what you want the class to do at each particular time. Also, if your students happen to ask an important question, for example, you can sometimes turn it into a task for all of them to try for a couple of minutes, before you answer the question. (This sometimes gives you the luxury of a couple of minutes to get your own answer ready).

Getting students to do things in lectures

The most effective learning methods are student-centred activities and it is a good idea to consider integrating activities into large-group lectures and to get the students doing something. When planning a lecture think of what students will be *doing* during the lecture. Don't worry too much about what *you* will be doing; plan to get your students' brains engaged. Get them making decisions, guessing causes of phenomena, trying out applying ideas, solving problems and so on. They'll learn more from what *they* do than from what you tell them.

If the room is suitable get them working together. Consider inviting volunteers down to the front of the lecture theatre to take part in an experiment or demonstration.

Hint: ***involving students as much as possible in the lecture not only has the benefit of more active learning but can save you time. Consider passing responsibility for quality assurance of your lectures to your students by paying them for spotting mistakes you make or for offering suggestions for improvement. For example, you could pay £1 for the first email you receive after each lecture identifying a specific mistake or suggesting a particular improvement. You could start the next lecture off by paying the students and announcing the reason for each payment. Not only do students pay more attention to the lecture, but also the quality of your lectures can be improved for very little outlay!***

Teaching strategically

In the end it is as well to recognise that many of today's students are strategic in their approach to learning. Much of the literature focuses on how we can move students away from this approach towards deeper learning. This book, however, is about teaching smarter. If students are strategic learners, focusing only on those activities directly relating to assessment, then let's be strategic teachers. If you wish students to attend lectures then you need to ensure that each lecture relates to an element of assessment. If you wish students to engage with learning in large groups then design activities in lectures which are related to assessment. If you use examples in lectures that derive directly from the assignment students are more likely to listen. If you ask students to draft answers to exam questions or to follow through an assessment-related worked exercise with you they will be more likely to do so than if they see no connection with the assessment. Purists will object to the idea of 'teaching to the test' but students will engage and learn if you do so.

How can we effectively integrate and use feedback?

The importance of feedback in lectures

It is important for us to know during a lecture if students have got the point so that we can either move on to the next point or give further explanation. The more frequent the feedback from students and the richer that feedback, the more opportunity there is for us to alter the pace and direction of the lecture. Such is the importance of feedback that many institutions have invested in electronic keypads and other sophisticated feedback systems. Whilst advocates of these systems point to their ability to immediately calculate quantitative data, such as proportions of students giving each response, there is of course the overhead of set-up and the associated potential for technical failure. They also represent a buffer between students and lecturers which in most cases is unnecessary and undesirable. There are in fact many easy (and cheap!) ways to integrate and use feedback in lectures which require no set-up of equipment. Non-technical solutions can include voting by a show of hands, setting written tests, using Post-its, conducting small-group discussions and implementing verbal questions and answers.

Questions and answers in lectures

Questions and answers work both ways. During your lecture you've got the opportunity to help your students to think, and asking them questions helps them to make sense of the topic and lets you know how well they are doing so, alerting you to areas where they are not yet succeeding to get their heads round the subject material being addressed. Allowing, and indeed encouraging, students to ask you questions helps you to find out what your students still need from you on their journey towards achieving the intended learning outcomes.

Getting students to ask you questions

What *not* to do: namely just ask "any questions?" now and then. Why not? Usually there will be no response, especially if you ask this towards the end of your lecture. Students are likely simply to take your question as a sign to start packing up their pens, handouts, and kit.

Also, when students *do* take advantage of your offer to respond to their questions, you will tend to get questions from the relatively confident students, who aren't usually the ones who need most to have their questions answered. On the whole, students are shy of asking questions in lectures, not least because of the fear that they may ask a 'stupid' question and then feel embarrassed. Even when we assure them of "Better to feel stupid for a moment than to remain ignorant for a lifetime", voicing a question in a lecture is a risky prospect for most students. That's why they tend to come up to you at the end and ask their questions individually – but with schedules to keep, and the next class coming in shortly, that's not an ideal alternative in practice.

Some suggestions for when students do ask you questions in lectures include:

- Repeating the question to everyone – many may not have heard it, and your answer won't make any sense if this is the case.
- Even if it *is* a stupid question, don't make it's owner feel stupid – just answer it quickly and kindly.
- If you don't know the answer, don't make one up – say that you'll find out, or ask if anyone else has the answer.

Hint: ***a useful way of getting questions from a large group of students is to pass some Post-its around. Ask all the students to jot down any questions they have, one per Post-it, and either to pass them down to you or to stick them on a wall or door on their way out of the lecture. You can then gauge which questions are the most prevalent ones, and answer them in your next lecture, and note also what the other questions tell you about how the overall learning is progressing in the group.***

A variation of this is the 'paper shower'. Students write their question on a piece of paper, screw up the paper into a ball and throw it at the lecturer!

What to do if you can't answer a question

First of all, if it's a question that your students don't actually *need* to know an answer to, say so. "Interesting, but not actually needed for your course" and so on. If it is a valuable question give yourself time to think. Repeat the question to everyone, as other students may not have heard it. Consider saying "This is a really good question. How many of *you* can respond to this?" and look for volunteers. Quite often, there will be someone there who is willing to answer it. At the very least this extra time is enough to give you a chance to think about how you may respond. If you still don't know the answer consider breaking it down into smaller bits. Then start by responding to one of the bits where you *do* have something to say. Finally, admit that at this point in time you don't have an answer to the question, but you will find one by the time of the next lecture. Invite the student who asked the question to jot it down on a Post-it, with their email address, so that you know *exactly* what the question was, and can respond to the questioner directly as soon as you've located an answer. Whatever you do don't try to make an answer up! If it turns out to be wrong, or if you get stuck in the process, you will soon have the full attention of all of the students – not what you really want at this stage!

Getting students to answer your questions

In large-group lectures in particular, students can be quite reticent about answering your questions. They may fear looking stupid, or 'being caught out' when they haven't been paying attention, and so on.

Here are some 'don'ts' for asking questions in your lectures.

- Don't ask the whole class a question, then simply answer it yourself. That just causes the class not to take your questions seriously.
- Don't pick on the same students each time you ask a question – for example, the ones who happen to have eye contact with you. That just discourages students to look at you!
- Don't just pick on students near to you – that allows those at the back to become even more switched-off than they may be already.
- Don't choose a student and *then* ask your question – that causes everyone else not even to try to think of an answer to your question.

Question, pause, pounce!

A good way to ask students questions in your lecture is by using this three-stage approach:

1 Ask the question.

2 Wait for enough time for most students to be ready to give at least some level of answer.
3 Pounce – pick a student at random.

This means more students think of an answer – their learning is more active. Don't, however, intimidate students. When you pick a student who can't (or won't) answer a particular question, move on fairly quickly to another student. If students come to *fear* the prospect of being asked a question in a large-group situation, they may well opt not to attend at all!

Hint: ***where possible, show your questions on-screen, so that students can see it as well as hear it. It also makes the questions seem more important to students, and they're more likely to take on board that these are the questions that they need to become able to answer.***

Hint: ***if you're issuing handouts in your lecture, it only takes a minute or two to pencil onto (say) the top right-hand corner of each copy a number, 1 to 257 for example. You can then ask students to note the number on their handout, and also to notice the numbers on their neighbours' handouts. You can then ask your question, pause for a moment, then say "Whoever has handout number 78, please?". You may notice this particular student 'shrinking', but people close to the student will point out the person concerned. Then when you've asked your next question, you can return to the owner of handout 78 and ask "Now you pick a number between 1 and 257, please", and from now on it isn't a matter of you picking on particular students to answer your questions – they now have ownership of the process.***

Hint: ***a simple feedback system which offers more options involves issuing students with four coloured cards labelled A–D. Frequent multiple-choice questions can be displayed at the front of the lecture theatre with colour-coded options which students answer by holding up the card which corresponds to the selected option. By using carefully designed questions, the lecturer can easily identify problems in student learning and address these problems immediately. Questions can of course be quite complex, requiring an informed guess or eliciting student opinions. The coloured cards can also be used as a signalling system by students (e.g. red card – "I haven't grasped the concept yet", green card – "Yes, I'm following").***

How can you contingency plan?

Time management

When planning a timetabled one-hour lecture slot it is important not to regard it as 60 minutes worth of content. Within the notional one-hour lecture you need, as a minimum, to consider allowing time for:

- the preceding class to vacate the room;
- students to arrive and settle in;
- explaining the intended outcomes;
- answering student questions;
- dwelling on points that need additional explanation;
- revisiting the intended outcomes;
- leaving the room ready for the next class;
- allowing time for your students to move to their next class.

It is therefore sensible to plan a maximum of 40 minutes for the 'delivery' part of your lecture. In practice, however, 40 minutes is still too long for you to 'deliver' and too long for your students to 'receive' as concentration spans are much shorter than 40 minutes.

It is a good idea to break the lecture down into shorter elements, perhaps four elements of ten minutes each, and to alternate between talking to students and getting students to do things – for example making notes, asking you questions, answering the questions you ask them. The advantages of this approach are:

- It should take far less time for you to prepare two, ten-minute talks than a continuous 60-minute monologue.
- It is easier for you to 'cut and paste' activities from one lecture to another if time runs out or if you find you have time available to fill in a session.
- It gives you a chance in the lecture to catch your breath, regain your composure, and plan what exactly to do next.

There are, of course, three possible scenarios when it comes to time-management in a lecture – that the planned session will finish exactly on time; that you will come to the end of your planned session early; or that the session will overrun.

Finishing early

Don't worry about finishing early! Students actually *like* lectures which finish early now and then. However, it is a good idea to have something in reserve. Simple, effective activities which take little time to prepare include:

- Asking a set of short, sharp quiz questions on your lectures to date with the group.
- Giving out Post-its, asking students to write any questions they would like to ask about the subject on them, and to then pass the Post-its down to you. Choose which questions to answer to the whole group until the time is used up.
- Putting up a slide of a past exam question on the topic you've been covering, and explaining to students a little about what was be expected in answers to that question.
- Giving a brief overview of what's coming next – for example showing the students the intended learning outcomes for the next couple of lectures.

Running out of time

There will always be occasions when the session progresses more slowly than you envisaged. Fire alarms, technical problems, or other factors outside of your control can collude to slow progress. When this happens it is important not to overrun. Whilst students will rarely complain if a lecture finishes a little early, they are less forgiving of lecturers who overrun. Do not fall into the trap of going at a rate of knots at the end of your session to get through the remaining content. It is far better when faced with this situation to identify a good stopping place, do your closing bit and stop.

Planning for nerves

Even very experienced lecturers can be nervous working with large groups. The best thing you can do is to prepare for the worst. Three things you can do which take very little time to prepare are to:

- Print off an outline of your lecture in case you lose your place. If you are using PowerPoint, print off a handout for yourself so you can be reminded which slide is coming next.
- Prepare an overhead that you can use at any point in the lecture asking students to jot down the two most important things they've learned so far from your lecture/s and compare these with those students sitting closest to them. Then ask for volunteers to tell you what they chose. This often helps you to gain a feel for exactly what has been happening in *their* minds up to that point, as well as giving you the welcome opportunity to compose your thoughts.
- Smile, rather than sweat! Even if inside you're quite tense, it's best to give the impression of being cool even when you're not. You'll notice that at least some of the students will smile back – this should immediately make you feel better.

Technology failure

As you become increasingly dependent upon technology in the lecture theatre the likelihood that the technology will let you down becomes highly probable. Network unavailability, software freezing, bulb failure or pieces of missing kit are now features of many large-group sessions. Six things to do that take little effort are:

- Arrive five minutes early for the session and try to set-up equipment before the students arrive.
- If you're unsure about the equipment, arrange for a technician to be available for the first five minutes of a class and have a direct contact number that you can use if needed during the session.
- It's a good idea *always* to have a discussion task ready and waiting. Ask your students to talk to those sitting next to them – give them a decision to reach, a problem to solve, and so on. Then when they're all busy and eyes are off you, you can try to rescue the technology.
- Ask for help. "Anyone know how to fix this please?" quite often brings a competent volunteer from the floor.
- If it's towards the end of a session, wind up. Remind your students of the intended learning outcomes, and promise to cover anything important that remains outstanding on a future occasion (your students won't mind you stopping early).
- Always carry a whiteboard pen with you!

The thing *not* to do is to struggle for ages, with the undivided attention of the whole group. The technology will let you down. Accept it, but don't allow it to throw you. Remember, your main value to your students is as a supporter of their learning through formative feedback and not as a disseminator of content. Visual aids and content can be posted on the web afterwards. When all else fails talk to your students – they may even enjoy the novelty of a lecture without technology!

Ten tactics for motivating students in your lectures

Do you sometimes look round at students' faces in your lectures, and ask yourself 'Is there anyone actually there?' Sometimes this is because your students are lacking in motivation. The following suggestions may help you to generate some motivation.

1 *Tell them about what's in it for them.* Think of the benefits they should derive from attending this particular lecture. How will it help them within the big

picture? What will they take away with them, that they wouldn't have got if they hadn't attended? How will being present at this lecture make their future lives easier? Sometimes, you'll have to work out how to respond to 'What's in it for me?' by thinking quite hard about what exactly your students should be getting out of the lecture. Sometimes, the intended learning outcomes will lend themselves to identifying the benefits of being present.

2 *Link each lecture forward to assessment.* Most students are driven by assessment. If they know they will get marks for something in due course, they will pay more attention to it. In fact, each lecture *should* link onward to assessment in one way or another – whether leading towards an exam question possibility or a coursework assignment. Assessment should link firmly to students' evidence of achievement of the intended learning outcomes, so you should be able to comment on the links when you talk about these outcomes at the beginning and end of each lecture.
3 *Smile!* Show enthusiasm – not just for the subject but also for the students. Make them feel welcome. Help them to feel that you are pleased to see them. Enthusiasm is infectious! If *you* look bored with the subject you're going to lecture on, that won't do anything for your students' motivation.
4 *Make lectures an active learning experience for your students.* They will remember what they *do* in your lectures much better than what you tell them. Plan at least three things for them to do in any hour. Bring in variety – something to do on their own, something to do in little buzz groups, and some questions for them to answer (for example in an oral quiz).
5 *Ring the changes.* Don't have students doing the same sort of thing for too long in any lecture. Concentration spans are measured in minutes, not hours. Motivation is often inversely proportional to boredom. When students say "The time flew by" you will know you're winning, and that they are more likely to look forward to your lectures.
6 *Help students to* make *notes, not just* take *notes.* Just copying things down from the screen – or from what you say – is a very passive business. Students can *take* notes without the subject really passing through their conscious minds. Get them to *make* notes, for example by giving them a couple of minutes now and then to make their own summaries of what you've been explaining to them, or to try out what they've learned on case-study examples or problems.
7 *Make it worth their while being there.* They should take away with them more than just a pristine handout. Their motivation will increase if they feel that they've actually achieved something during each lecture. Aim to allow students to make sense of concepts and ideas *during* the actual lecture, rather than hoping that they will go away and make sense of things in their own time.
8 *Make the best use of a whole group being together.* For example, use lectures to find out what questions students have and answer them. This is actually

much more efficient for you than explaining the same answers to different students at different times. It's also fairer, as those students who prefer to ask questions privately could otherwise become advantaged over those who don't. Use lectures to answer all the important questions, so that people who didn't even realise that they didn't yet know the answer to a question are also helped.

9 *Don't pretend that every part of the subject is extremely interesting!* All subject have their less interesting bits. Admit to your students that certain parts are difficult – even tedious – but explain why they *need* to master these parts to be able to move on to more interesting and more important areas. Students' motivation sometimes increases when they realise that finding something tedious or difficult is not at all unexpected to you. It helps them to appreciate that you're on their side and helping them with their learning, not just expecting them to be enthusiastic about everything without question.

10 *Come to a definite conclusion towards the end of each lecture.* Don't just stop when time runs out. Help students to feel that they have really achieved something in each lecture. Remind them of the intended learning outcomes for that lecture, and check to what extent they now feel that they've achieved them. Don't be concerned when there are some outcomes that they haven't yet achieved – come back to these in future lectures. Some things need several attempts before they begin to make sense – let students know this is perfectly normal.

Conclusion

Designed and delivered correctly, the large lecture offers a great opportunity to efficiently and effectively engage students in active learning.

When designing large-group lectures it is useful to use the following checklist:

1 What are we trying to achieve?
2 What do students need to learn?
3 How is this lecture linked to assessment?
4 What are students going to do?
5 How are we going to use feedback to check if students are learning?

It's a good idea not to try to put too much content into a lecture. It's better to get students thinking deeply about a couple of important things, than to tell them about half-a-dozen things and lose their attention. The initial investment of time spent preparing a large-group lecture can pay dividends in the long run, although this time is far better spent on designing student activities, on finding simple ways to get students to recall concepts and on gaining feedback than on professional visual aids and lengthy monologues.

This chapter has sought to offer some suggestions that may make your lectures more effective and more efficient to design and deliver. Ultimately, however, lectures would be dull for students if we all approached them in exactly the same ways, and they need to fit comfortably with your own personality, so overall the best plan is to approach large-group teaching in your own way, to try to enjoy yourself but to keep checking on how your students are finding your approach.

6

Dealing with disruptive students

This chapter addresses the following questions:

- Which student behaviours are disruptive to student learning?
- How can we prevent disruptive student behaviour?
- How can we effectively deal with disruptive behaviour when it occurs?

Why do disruptive students cause an increasingly significant problem?

Things have changed! Among the changes over the last two or three decades, the following can be regarded as causes of the increases in the occurrence of disruptive students behaviours in universities and colleges.

1 *There is much less discipline in schools than previously*. This is partly because teachers are no longer able to discipline pupils using the kinds of corporal punishment remembered by many older people! Society's view of such things has changed, and pupils nowadays know that any teachers who step out of line on such matters are likely to be putting their jobs at risk, and may even end up in the law courts. Unruly behaviours in school are much more common that hitherto, and some of this carries forward into post-compulsory education.

2 *Parents and guardians are less likely to be supportive to educators regarding disruptive behaviour*. Many regard it as none of their business, and believe that educational institutions should be able to handle such issues.

3 *In many parts of the world, including in the UK, students are now consumers of higher education*. Indeed, the costs of higher education are increasingly met by students themselves through fees and loans (and by their parents), and in line with general trends in consumerism, students are more likely to complain when they feel that they are not being treated properly, and sometimes this manifests itself in the form of disruptive behaviours.

4 *Students are more aware of their rights*. And more likely to be confident to speak out and complain if they feel they are being unfairly treated.

What else has changed?

One significant change, which contributes to increasing levels of disruption, is the lack of opportunity for teachers to build up a positive relationship with large groups of students. In busy modular timetables, it is common for an individual teacher just to see a given large group of students for perhaps a single hour in a week, and for the students themselves to be in quite different groups in different modules or combinations of teaching pathways. Therefore, it is no longer possible to build up the sort of teacher-student relationship which was possible when an individual teacher oversaw a significant chunk of their learning experience.

What is disruptive behaviour?

Disruptive behaviour is any behaviour that interferes with your ability to teach or other students' ability to engage in learning. Common disruptive behaviours include talking when you or others are speaking; arriving late for class and leaving class early; inappropriately demanding individual attention; constantly interrupting; challenging your authority; being inattentive, sleeping or using mobile phones in your class; monopolising classroom discussions; rambling and constantly arguing with the tutor or other students.

More extreme examples of disruptive behaviour which you may have to deal with at some point include verbal abuse; drunken and drug-related behaviour; the forming of romantic attachments; harassment or stalking; threats to harm themselves or others and physical violence.

Why are students disruptive?

There are many reasons why students might be disruptive. McKeachie (1994) categorises the disruptive as:

- angry, aggressive students;
- attention seekers and those who dominate discussions;
- inattentive or unprepared students;
- flattering students;
- discouraged and defeated students;
- students with a million excuses;
- students who want the 'truth' or even the 'right answer'.

There are occasions when some students are deliberately disruptive, but more often a perpetrator may be completely unaware that their behaviour is interfering with your teaching or with other students' learning. Other behaviours may appear to be intentional but can in fact be a result of factors beyond a student's control. Students have lives outside your classroom and various aspects may affect their behaviour in your class.

Some of your students may not be particularly interested in your subject and may find your classes unstimulating. When considering how to deal with disruptive students it is therefore timely to think about student motivation and effective pedagogy. You could have been pitching the session at too high a level and have lost some students as a result. Conversely, some students may feel the session is too low level or that you are patronising them. If you invest time in considering how to engage our students intellectually and perhaps even emotionally in learning you may find disruption is reduced. However, even the most effective lecturers will sometimes experience students who are disruptive so it is useful to plan for this and to be proactive in considering how we might encourage appropriate behaviour in our students. All disruption can potentially interfere with student learning and it is therefore important that we deal with it effectively and efficiently when it occurs.

Contexts for disruption

The vast majority of teachers' problems with disruptive students seem to occur in large-group contexts. This is partly because, from the students' viewpoint, there is strength in numbers and if a lecture group becomes restless it is relatively easy for that restlessness to erupt into outright disruption. From the teacher's point of view, large-group disruption (even when just one or two students are actually behaving in a disruptive way) is much more hard to take than small-group or one-to-one outbreaks. This is because the audience is so much larger, and whatever happens will be remembered by everyone present.

Small-group disruption is much less serious, as there is more opportunity for the disruption to be talked through with everyone present. One-to-one disruptive behaviour is relatively rare, not least because a student is less likely to risk getting seriously on the wrong side of an academic, particularly if there is a witness sitting somewhere close by. It can indeed be useful to arrange encounters with potentially disruptive students where there is just such a witness – a colleague working at another desk in the room, for example. With one-to-one incidents, this also has the advantage that there is a witness present who can if necessary give an objective view of what happened, avoiding the 'one person's word against another's' situation.

Preventing disruptive behaviour

Perhaps the best thing you can do to address disruptive student behaviour is to attempt to prevent it through good teaching and by creating an environment in which it is unlikely to occur. There are five characteristics of a supportive environment to minimise disruptive behaviour:

- control;
- clarity;
- credibility;
- consistency;
- care.

You must be seen to be in control of the class. It is possible to demonstrate to students that you are in control of the class whilst still involving them in activities, asking and answering questions and sharing their experiences and viewpoints. In fact using interactive teaching methods can help to prevent distracting behaviours by involving students in the class.

For students who have little interest in your subject or difficulties in understanding it is particularly important to be clear and explicit about your goals for each session, so consider starting each one by explaining the intended learning outcomes. It is also useful to tell students how you expect them to behave in class. Set standards high and show students how to meet them; expect good behaviour.

Your students are more likely to listen to you if they regard you as credible, so prepare thoroughly for each class to ensure that they will have confidence in you and will trust you. Ideally you should be able to answer student questions, but if you don't know the answer to a question admit it and ensure that students get access to the information as soon as possible. In terms of your credibility it's probably more important that you are organised, enthusiastic and have good presentation skills. This goes a long way to ensuring you keep students' attention focused and helps prevent distracting classroom behaviour such as lateness and talking. Be consistent in your dealings with students and in how you deal with any classroom difficulties. Students like to know where they stand and what the 'rules of the game' are.

Finally, try where possible to use students' names. Students work better when they feel that their lecturers care about them, so avoid the use of sarcasm or cynicism and share your passion for your subject.

How to generate 'presence'

It is worth thinking of those colleagues who never seem to suffer from outbreaks of disruptive behaviour, in particular in large-group student contexts. How do they avoid disruption? Possible answers include:

- they are teaching subjects which their students find interesting;
- they are good at nipping disruption in the bud;
- when some disruption does occur, they manage to 'weather the storm' calmly,

and with good humour;
- they simply have 'presence'.

Perhaps the last of these, 'presence', is really important. We can all think of people who have this – and people who lack it. Perhaps also are there are some actions we can take which can increase our presence? Someone who has 'presence' seems to have to do very little to get the attention of a large group at the beginning of a lecture, or to retain attention right at the end. It is, however, much easier to list some symptoms of *lack of* presence than it is to describe how to achieve presence. Lack of presence may be characterised by one or more symptoms, including:

- Lack of sufficient eye contact with large groups of students. For example, if a lecturer is not looking at the class sufficiently, he or she might not notice the first signs of unrest in the group, and the students heading towards a disruptive outburst may feel that they are unlikely to be challenged. Eye contact is very important, not just in keeping the attention of a lecture group, but as an aid to conveying the meaning of words, slides and overheads, and for checking that the audience is actually getting the message, then repeating or re-explaining as necessary on the basis of 'reading' the audience.
- Lack of confidence. Confidence comes with experience, and with knowing the subject thoroughly before starting to teach it. However, the latter is no substitute for the former – a really confident teacher can in practice 'wing it' very effectively when teaching a new subject, not least by turning the lecture into a *shared* learning journey. In other words, students' trust in a teacher seems to be more to do with the teacher's perceived confidence than in their knowledge or authority in the subject.
- Lack of skills in starting a lecture well. Getting a lecture going is a balancing act, as there will often be potential triggers of disruption, not least students arriving late and settling in unduly noisily. Any blundering in handling these opening problems will flavour the rest of the session.
- Lack of skills in keeping students' attention right at the very end of the session. When a lecturer signals that the session is about to close, there is a natural tendency for students to close books, rustle papers, shut files, start to pack bags, and so on. If the lecturer meanwhile is continuing to talk to the whole group, this signals that such behaviour is tolerated, and memories of this may subconsciously spill over and affect students' behaviours at future sessions. Ways need to be found to keep attention right at the end, such as getting students themselves to answer some questions, or by giving vital clues regarding exactly what the class should really remember from what has been discussed, for example hinting at how to go about a likely exam question.

One aspect of 'presence' seems to be a kind of serenity – in other words, the feeling that nothing at all is going to really rattle or upset us. This can indeed be an inhibitor to outbreaks of disruptive behaviour, since if our students believe that we will take any such outbreaks calmly in our stride, it becomes less attractive to indulge in such disruption.

Who can we learn from and who has experience of avoiding disruption?

It is worth thinking of contexts where disruptive behaviour is very rare, or is not tolerated when it does happen. Examples of people who have their own ways and systems for minimising and dealing with disruptive behaviour include:

- Prison staff. For example, education officers in the prison service. If you have the chance to talk to such officers, they will usually make you feel that your own problems with disruptive behaviour are small by comparison, but they will also help you to see how systems and environments can be designed where it is possible to nip disruption in the bud as soon as there is a whiff of it in the air. The most scary tales they tell are usually of actual violence – between inmates, or even toward staff. Such staff can also give you sound advice about not stepping in between people who are fighting, and getting other people out of the way to safety, and so on.
- Police persons. They too often have to sort out disruption which has gone out of control, and have sound advice to offer regarding fighting, shouting, and extreme disruptive behaviour. In addition, they have to be able to protect themselves against accusations of handling the situation badly, and must ensure that any incidents are properly witnessed, by people who can if necessary testify that the actions taken were appropriate.
- Military personnel. Stories of disruptive behaviour in military training contexts are rare, and it would seem that a combination of 'presence' and 'authority', plus well-established ground rules and codes of conduct, minimises outbreaks of disruption.
- School teachers. Talking to friends who teach in school – particularly at secondary level – usually reminds us that the problems we may encounter with disruptive behaviour in post-compulsory education are much less serious than our school-teacher friends sadly have to take for granted.

One common factor shared by prison staff, police persons, military personnel and school teachers is that they work in environments where things are 'compulsory', unlike higher education. In other words, they have sanctions at their disposal which are not available in post-compulsory education, where the only real sanction becomes exclusion – which is often quite hard to achieve, and can't be achieved quickly enough to be a significant deterrent to full-flow disruptors.

Dealing with disruptive behaviour

Of course, even when you take steps to prevent disruptive behaviour you can never guarantee a disruption-free class. Generally, it is as well to give any sort of disruptive student the minimum attention necessary because time focused on disruptive behaviour is time that is not being spent on facilitating learning. Also, there is a danger of drawing other students into the situation who will the escalate the disruption. The golden rule of dealing with disruptive behaviour is never to do anything that will make the situation worse. Below are suggestions for dealing with the most common types of disruptive behaviour.

Dealing with noisy students

Students holding side conversations, using mobile phones or MP3 players can be quite off-putting for you and for other students. A direct approach of "Please don't use your mobile phone" can often be the most effective. Consider starting the class with something like "Please switch all phones off, we're about to start." This not only sets the ground rules but also clearly indicates that the session has begun. It's not a good idea to embarrass students who are talking or assume that their conversation isn't related to what is being discussed in class. You may therefore wish to avoid direct confrontation, in which case the following are often successful:

- Stop talking in mid-sentence and look in a non-aggressive way at the student making the noise. Peer pressure may quieten them.
- Try speaking more quietly. This causes the noisy students to become more obvious in contrast and other students may ask them to quieten down.
- Make direct eye contact with the student/s so that they know you can see them.
- Direct a question to the area in which the noisy students are sitting. This focuses attention on that area of the class.
- Try physically moving to the part of the room where the students are and continue to lead the class whilst standing next to them.
- If you hear a student make an interesting comment you could respond to it, thereby encouraging comments from other students.
- Consider legitimising the chatting by breaking the class into mini-discussion groups.

Dealing with inattentive students

Students who don't pay attention are not necessarily disruptive and you should weigh up the benefits of interceding before acting. If you decide you would like to increase a student's attentiveness it is a good idea to try to make eye contact with them. You may also find that students are suddenly more attentive if you ask them a question, if you explicitly relate the topic to assessment or keep them active.

Dealing with late arrivers

This is one of those matters which is high on most lecturers' list of problems. How you handle late-comers will be one of the things that sets the whole tone of your classes. The following suggestions may help you to weigh up the pros and cons of a variety of tactics, and to choose what will work best for you.

Don't forget that sometimes students have good reasons for being late. There may have been a transport problem. They may have just come from a previous lecture on a distant part of the campus – or another campus altogether. Their previous lecture may have over-run – this isn't *their* fault. Avoid saying anything irretrievable. It could be that this was the first time ever that the late-comer had been late and/or it might have been unavoidable, but they still plucked up the courage to come in. Remember that the late-comer has at least got to you.

If you are too hard on late-comers, they may well decide simply not to come at all next time they're late for your sessions. This may well cause you more problems, not least that regular late-comers who become regular absentees are naturally much more likely to fail your course or module, and this reflects on you even when it's not your fault. Recognise that at least some disruption is inevitable. It's usually best not to simply carry on as though no one was making their late way into the class. At the very least some of the other students may well miss something you said, distracted by the late-comer's entrance. Sometimes it's best simply to pause till the late-comer is settled in. In any case, a few extra moments to gather your own thoughts can often be useful. When there are repeated disturbances through the arrival of successive late-comers, the majority of the students often have their own ways of showing their disapproval concerning the disruption, sparing you from having to do anything.

If students are habitually arriving late for your class and distracting students who arrive on time, then let students know that the first five minutes of each class will cover material relating directly to the assignment. You don't then need to make special efforts to brief late-comers about what they may have missed – and indeed if those without good reasons for being late begin to realise that they are missing useful things, they will tend to try to be more punctual in future.

Dealing with early leavers

This same approach of including something relevant to assessment can be applied to the last five minutes of class to encourage students not to leave early. If students see the value in being there they are more likely to make the effort. If this doesn't have any effect on persistent early leavers (or late attenders) then you need to tread carefully. You may wish to state clearly your expectations for attendance, but equally you may wish not to risk alienating the students. Whatever you do, don't waste time at the beginning or end of the session discussing excuses as this is unfair to the rest of the class and is unproductive.

Dealing with domineering students

Some students can overpower the group and inhibit the contributions and learning of others. It's your responsibility to manage the group, without alienating these students or disrupting learning. In a small group, make eye contact with every member and then ask the domineering student to ensure that everyone in the group has contributed to the discussion. In a large class establish eye contact with the domineering student and then thank them for their contribution. Then try asking someone in another part of the room to speak. If the student persists in dominating the discussion summarise their point and ask others to speak, or indicate that you are ready to move on by starting to prepare for the next activity.

Dealing with rambling students

Some students can regularly wander around and off the subject. Clearly this can detract from the learning experience of other students. It is important to try to refocus the student's attention by restating relevant points and asking the student to summarise their main point. Try directing questions to the group, perhaps using visual aids to bring the discussion back on track.

Dealing with distressed students

Whilst it is good to be empathetic, it is not appropriate for you to become a student's counsellor. It is not your responsibility to offer therapy but to manage the situation to enable the rest of the class to get on with their learning. Refer students with emotional, psychological or financial trouble to the appropriate counsellors.

Dealing with challenges to your authority

Some students may make a habit of disagreeing with everything you say. You should consider recognising their opinions, pulling out any valid points and restating them before moving, on perhaps drawing the rest of the group into the discussion. It is important not to be sidetracked or to enter into an argument. It may be best to arrange to discuss the issues with the student out of class time. Be willing to explain, but not necessarily to defend, your position.

Dealing with disruptive students online

Possibly because of the difficulty in interpreting emotions, disruptions to online classes can be challenging to manage. Disruption can be direct such as abusive emails, or less direct such as a student posting material which offends some others. Following are some methods for dealing with disruptive students online:

- Delete any inappropriate postings on the discussion board.
- Phone or email the disruptive student and objectively inform the student of the problem and how they were disruptive.
- Explain what the possible consequences will be if they continue to be disruptive.
- For a persistent offender consider blocking the student from posting in a forum or removing that student from the group.
- Save any postings for future reference.

Ineffective ways to deal with disruption

Most of us learn the hard way that there are some avenues which are NOT advisable when dealing with disruption in class.

1 *Reacting aggressively*. Although you may find that in the short term shouting at students works, in the longer term students may lose respect for you if the only way you can maintain control of a class is by losing control of yourself. It is not a good idea to try to intimidate students as this may lead to a stand-off where students not wishing to lose face may challenge you further. At the very least you are likely to reduce their engagement.

2 *Ignoring the disruption*. It is inadvisable to ignore or give in to unacceptable behaviour as you may find that the disruption increases and you risk losing control of the class. It's also not generally a good idea to resort to sarcasm or embarrassing students, as you may harm your credibility and lose respect.

3 *Punishing the non-disruptive students*. If you refuse to carry on until a couple of chattering students quieten down then this penalises the non-disruptive students. Equally, locking the door five minutes into class time stops chronic late comers but also penalises the student who may have an unavoidable reason for being late.

A far better way to deal with disruption is to focus on maintaining control without resorting to aggression or sarcasm.

Don't let a crisis turn into a drama!

This is the golden rule in dealing with disruptive students, particularly in large-group contexts like lectures. This is perhaps best illustrated by a case study.

> One Thursday, Dr Smith was lecturing to a large class in a research-led university. He was teaching a rather difficult (and not particularly interesting) mathematical area of an engineering topic, and his students were getting fed up, both with Dr Smith and the subject. Dr Smith himself was rather more interested in his research than his teaching at the time of the incident and was somewhat stretched by also getting a funding bid in on time, so his patience was not at its optimum.
>
> When he turned to the board to write a rather cumbersome equation for the students to copy down, a student whistled. He turned round but could not see who had whistled. When he resumed writing the equation, the whistle was heard again. He again turned round, but still could not distinguish the culprit. He turned round quickly enough at the next occurrence of the whistle, and caught the student who had whistled. He was quite cross at this point, and asked the student to leave the lecture. The student refused.

As you may imagine, this crisis had turned into a drama. There was no going back. In fact, Dr Smith had to be taken off the course concerned, as uppermost in the minds of that set of students would be the incident from that Thursday. The pivotal point was Dr Smith asking the student to leave – and the student refusing. This was an irreversible step. In an instant, even many of the students who actually found the whistling juvenile and irritating tended to side with the offender. If the student *had* left, the incident may have receded away from the consciousness of the student group over time, but the student still remained. Short of getting the university's security staff to take the student away there was no turning back, and that in itself would have constituted an irreversible step.

It is not surprising that something rather dramatic, such as the incident above, is likely to be considerably more memorable to the students than the rather dry and boring topic that was being covered in the lecture. The fact that the result was for Dr Smith to be taken off the course was naturally taken as a victory by the students, even though most of them had little time for the offending student's behaviour that day. Perhaps the most important learning point from this story is that it only takes a second or two to get into an irreversible drama with a large group of students.

A ten step approach for dealing with disruptive students

1 Don't take the disruption personally	Focus on the distraction rather than on the student and don't take disruption personally. Students are often unaware that they are being disruptive. Your attitude will come across to your students so it is important that you remain positive and give students the benefit of the doubt. By remaining objective and not taking the situation personally, you can respond in a calm manner.
2 Stay calm	It is a good idea to take control of the situation before you become impatient, upset or irritated. You will be much more authoritative when you are perceived to be dealing with the distraction in a composed manner and when students believe that you like them. Don't become angry or sarcastic as this will make the situation worse. Save your energies for your teaching.
3 Decide when you will deal with the situation	It is very important that you allow students to save face where possible. The class will not always respond well if you put students down in front of others. If the nature of the disruption requires you to have a lengthy discussion with the student then arrange to meet after class. However, it is best to address most disruptive behaviours quickly and immediately as they arise.
4 Be polite	Don't get into an argument. It is far better to say "I'd like to continue with the class" or "It is important that you concentrate for the next few minutes" than "Don't talk when I'm talking."
5 Listen to the student	*Really* listen to what a disruptive student is saying. Where it is practicable let them finish and don't interrupt them. Put yourself in their shoes and try to understand what is lying behind the disruption.
6 Check you understand	Ask questions until you have enough information to understand the situation.
7 Decide what you're going to do	Think win-win but always prioritise the learning experience of the non-disruptive students.
8 Explain your decision to the student	Tell the students what you have decided, explain your rationale and check they understand.
9 Follow through	You must do what you said you would do! Don't threaten actions you are not prepared to carry out or that you are not able to ensure are carried out. Only in the most drastic of situations should you ask a student to leave the class – what will you do if a student refuses to leave? Only as a very last resort should you leave the class yourself. Don't threaten to do these things unless you are prepared to follow through on them.
10 Document your decisions	Where the disruption has resulted in significant action it is a good idea to document the nature of the disruption, your actions and the rationale for your decision. This will help you to reflect and evaluate.

Conclusion

No two classes are alike. Each class has its own personality and how you deal with disruptive behaviour may differ between classes. It's really helpful if you know all of your students' names because students are less likely to be disruptive if they know that you know them. Where you have tried unsuccessfully to resolve an issue in class it is usually best not to escalate the issue but to attempt to resolve it at a later time outside the classroom. If you are available to students outside class time and if you invite students to contact you with concerns and questions, both these actions can prevent many problems arising in class time.

Deal with each distraction objectively. If you're the only one who's being irritated by a particular behaviour, such as a student falling asleep, then that behaviour is only disruptive if you let it be. If you do anything in class to address a non-disruptive behaviour, you transform it into a disruption. You could therefore choose to ignore the behaviour. If the behaviour seriously annoys you, you could approach the student outside class and ask why they are doing it.

All the guidance in this chapter has been directed at dealing with non-threatening disruptive behaviour. However, should an incident occur in your class that causes you to fear for your safety or that of your students:

- Stay calm.
- Do not turn your back on the student.
- Do not touch the student.
- Call security.

Although incidents of this type are rare you never know when they might occur, so it is a good idea to always carry a mobile phone and to ensure that you know how to contact security.

Whilst it is useful to consider how you might deal with disruptions when they arise it is important not to worry overly about maintaining control. Interaction in a session is actually quite a good thing and the unpredictability of each class can enrich the students' and your experience. Although this chapter offers a range of suggestions for how to cope with different types of disruption, often the best course of action is the simplest; to ask the disruptive students to stop what they're doing. Finally, remember that most students are polite and helpful and want to learn!

7

Developing online learning

- Why is online learning not yet living up to its potential?
- What often goes wrong with online learning at present?
- What can online learning do – and what can't it do?
- What's the future of re-usable learning objects?

False dawns and failed prophets

Early on in the development of post-compulsory education theory, programmed learning was seen as the panacea for all ills. The traditional textbook was bound to be replaced by programmed learning texts, which would provide everything the student needed, without recourse to wider reading. These instructional manuals would revolutionalise student behaviour, by making everything crystal clear, with no creative ambiguity. If they chose the correct option at the foot of page 23, they would discover that they were right from the congratulatory message on page 78, but if they chose an incorrect option, they would find out on page 45 that they needed to do five further exercises before finding themselves once again at the foot of page 23. This rather pedestrian approach was essentially democratic in its ambitions, in that it was designed to avoid the lottery of students being taught by varied and potentially unreliable tutors, ensuring that everyone had equal opportunities to learn.

The principal problems with the programmed learning approach in print were the boredom, frustration and even anger felt by learners, who frequently felt that this depersonalised method of learning failed to give them any space for creativity and an individual approach. Moreover, they found themselves holding a book, with no feel for their progress. Until they'd finished the book they would never know what they were ignorant of. No wonder so many attempted to cheat by leapfrogging sections. Many fell by the wayside and gave up on such strange books, looking forward with anticipation to the next big thing – computer-based learning.

Meanwhile, video-recording came into being and the notion arose that all that was needed to cause high-quality learning to occur was to capture on video the best performances of podium stars. It was believed that recorded lectures by these people would be all that was needed for anyone to learn – at times of their own choosing, places of their choice, and with the potential to rewind the tape and view again and again the difficult bits until full understanding was achieved. It was imagined that teachers in all institutions would seize with relish this new addition to their repertoire, and make these recordings available to their students. An honourable exception to this trend was the UK's Open University, which recognised at the outset that learning by watching was never going to be a substitute for learning-by-doing and feedback, and which built interactive, print-based learning packages whereby the broadcast components were merely icing on the cake and meanwhile supported student learning via face-to-face group tutorials and residential summer schools.

In the early days of computers it was envisaged that computer-based learning would replace face-to-face tuition, and enthusiastic senior managers rubbed their hands in glee at the twin ideas both of saving on expensive teaching salaries and of taking control of curriculum delivery. Wild forecasts were made of the massive savings that would be brought about by economies of scale, by rationalising teaching materials, abolishing ownership of lecture notes, and of quality control born out of centralised direction.

Early books on the subject of computer-based learning envisaged students plugging in computers and receiving wisdom in cost-effective study carrels, with minimal teacher intervention. At the same time, computer-based marking using the falsely-named 'objective tests' was seen as the way to reduce the time delays and drudgery of hand-marked assignments. The essay was declared (prematurely) dead, and proponents of early computer-based assessment started to argue that all forms of assessment could be replaced by various types of automatic marking.

Optical mark readers, which enabled students (clumsily and inaccurately) to make marks with soft graphite pencils onto pre-printed templates which could then be scanned by optical readers, promised much. But the practicalities – with students using the wrong kind of pencil, crossing out their errors, and simply putting their marks in the wrong places – meant that the methodology had severe limitations.

Once again the intentions were honourable, with the ambition being to give students near-instant responses and to guarantee the reliability of the marking process whilst liberating teachers from the drudgery of detailed and repetitive hand-marking.

As with all visionary predictions, there were grains of truth and wisdom in these optimistic predictions. Online learning, as we now know it, has the capacity to be:

- Reliable.
- Efficient of time (especially when dealing with large numbers of students).
- Accountable.
- Accessible.
- Enabling (giving freedom of time, pace and place).
- Cost-effective.
- Auditable.
- Adaptable.
- Customisable.
- Flexible.
- Democratic.

In the next sections, we will discuss how you can turn dreams into actuality, but first we will visit some of the nightmares which currently exist.

What goes wrong with online learning now?

Race (2005) argues that, presently, the majority of online learning programmes are in fact little more than well-presented online information resources. What is essentially lacking is a means by which students can be encouraged and supported to be interactive; to be active learners rather than passive recipients of information. Knowledge transfer, as a concept, is essentially flawed because until students make sense of what they read, see and hear, by practical application, no such transfer can occur. Students cannot judge whether their knowledge has increased until they get feedback to confirm this.

Many problems arise with online learning currently, because insufficient thought is put into the development of curriculum materials. Unsophisticated users of virtual learning environments seem to think that all that is necessary is to put up into hyperspace copies of lecture notes, and imagine that students can be left to do the rest themselves. We should already know from decades of experience that students who merely acquire a copy of the notes from a missed lecture rarely learn anything like as much as those who were present at the event. Even those who put up video-streamed versions of their own lectures are in danger of falling into the same kinds of errors as early *aficionados* of programmed learning. An excessive focus on content at the expense of interactive processes means that course designers spend more time thinking about what is transmitted than how students receive it.

Similarly, course designers all too frequently fail to make the conceptual shift from learning from the page to learning from the screen, and therefore pay insufficient attention to design and layout. The worst forms of online learning require students to click through page after page of dreary-looking text, unrelieved by images, tables, and with nothing required other than passive receptivity. All this happens in an era when students have a highly selective approach to on-screen information, and have a channel-hopping reluctance to be bored by anything which fails to grab their attention. Effective online learning requires the expertise of three types of specialists: the content specialist, the educationalist with an understanding of how to design good interactive materials, and the technologist who can make it all happen. Rarely are all three kinds of expertise found in a single person, which is why online learning is necessarily best developed by teams or in institution-wide approaches where much training and support are provided. A kitchen-table, craft approach just doesn't do the trick. A generation accustomed to the high production values of fast, cross-cut movies and highly sophisticated computer games will have little patience with humble and mechanistic learning materials. For them, the message from online learning is only as good as the look of the medium.

Runaway technology, then signs of maturity

The technology supporting online learning has developed at a fast pace. The cost in real terms of computers, memory, servers, and other equipment has continued to decrease rapidly. The speed of the technology has multiplied quickly. The visual images on screens have vastly improved in quality. However, because online learning depends on technology, there has been a tendency for developments in online learning to be led by those well-versed in the developing information and communication technologies, rather than those well-trained in teaching and learning processes. For some years, to develop any virtual learning environment it was necessary to learn one or more of a range of authoring languages. Nowadays, however, virtual learning environments are evolving towards relatively well-defined platforms, which make it fairly straightforward for teachers (and learners) who are not versed in the technology to use them.

That said, most young learners in the developed world can be regarded as 'digital natives' – they have grown up with technology, and find it perfectly natural to play with it until they get it to do what they want it to do. Not for them the instruction manuals or online help files. Their teachers, however, are mostly still 'digital immigrants' – people who have not grown up with the technology, but who bravely venture into the new world of digital media. However, they bring with them habits from a previous era, where they don't feel comfortable with the media unless they have 'followed the directions' and can understand how it works.

In short, learners tend to be comfortable with virtual learning environments, while their teachers are much less relaxed. And added to this is that learners expect considerable sophistication, while their teachers find it hard to provide this.

At the present stage of development in online technologies, it could be argued that we have failed as yet to apply what we already know about how people learn, nor have we adequately brought in to online communication what we already know about how learners and teachers best communicate.

Perhaps the most visible symptom of online learning not yet having 'grown up' is that it is presently too often regarded by teachers as 'something different'. There are training days about implementing online learning, which tend to focus on the digital side of online learning but often miss out how online learning should integrate with lectures, tutorials, practical work and all the other elements making up an overall experience for learners. So for teachers online learning presently remains 'separate', yet for younger learners who are digital natives working in virtual learning environments comes naturally.

As with so many previous innovations, the view that online learning must be possible for just about everything has prevailed, and we have not yet really interrogated the potential of the medium in a bid to find out where to choose to exploit its benefits, and where to leave it well alone and continue with more traditional teaching and learning processes.

Online learning will have grown up properly when:

- it is used for what it does well, and not used for anything else;
- it is integrated seamlessly into the overall learning experience of students;
- teachers think more about the learning, and worry less about the technology.

Escaping from the dominant screen

Perhaps the first thing that comes to mind when thinking of any virtual learning environment is the screen. Mostly, these screens are quite small and can only contain a limited amount of information. However, just a mouse-click away is normally another screen – and what was on the previous screen all too readily evaporates away from learners' minds. Most people when learning from a screen also have books, articles, handouts, paper-based exercises and other aspects of traditional learning materials around them. In addition, they often have fellow-learners with whom they can interact, and teachers or trainers who can guide them and respond to their difficulties. However, because of the tendency for the design of online learning to be dominated by what appears on the screen, too little energy is spared for the design of supporting resources to accompany that screen. It is important to ensure that the medium is not used merely to feed information, but rather to cause learning to happen.

What can online learning do (and what can't it do)?

Online learning can help you to make your teaching work as follows. It can:

1. *Excite learners*, increasing their motivation to learn.
2. *Give learners plenty of learning-by-doing*, allowing them to learn online by practising, trial-and-error and repetition, and by giving them the opportunity to learn from mistakes in the comfort of privacy, finding out *why* particular choices or actions were wrong.
3. *Give learners instant feedback on choices or decisions*, again in the comfort of privacy, so that they are encouraged to play with ideas.
4. *Respond to where learners are in their learning*, for example, fast-tracking them forward through a programme where they are already mastering the content and slowing them down when they need more practice to fully grasp particular ideas or concepts.
5. *Save learners a lot of time searching for information*, by providing the relevant information to them on demand.
6. *Allow learners to test their understanding of what they are learning*, so that they gain a feel for the extent to which they are making sense of what they are learning, and have the opportunity to return to those parts which are proving more difficult to master.
7. *Build the confidence of those returning to learning*, allowing them to make multiple attempts at study elements.
8. *Offer flexible learning opportunities*, for those whose work, travel or caring commitments make it difficult for them to fit in with traditional attendance or assessment patterns.
9. *Provide the chance for learners who are time-rich to study at a faster pace*, than that which the normal academic year permits.
10. *Offer opportunities to disabled students*, particularly when care is taken in the design of inclusive virtual learning environments.
11. *Provide safe learning environments for those for whom college attendance feels risky*, for example, because of mental health problems, or where social constraints make it difficult for them to study face-to-face.
12. *Encourage reluctant learners*, those for whom classroom and text based study is an anathema.

However, online learning can't turn information into knowledge for learners. The process of turning information into knowledge can only be achieved by learners themselves through learning-by-doing, practice and trial and error, accompanied by feedback to aid the process of making sense of what is being learned. The problem is that it is often much easier to click the mouse and move on to the next screen of information, rather than stay and make sense of the last screen.

Online learning can, however, be designed so that learners cannot leave a particular screen without making a decision – for example choosing an option, entering some text or numbers, dragging and dropping something on the screen, and so on. Then they can be given feedback on what they have done, for example telling them whether or not it was the correct thing to do, or (more importantly) telling them what was wrong with the decision they made and leading them back to thinking again about the original agenda.

Here are some other things that online learning can't do. Online learning can't:

- Provide cash-strapped managers with quick fixes to resource constraints in the classroom.
- Do away with the necessity for an element of human interaction with learners to engage them in their learning.
- Stop students struggling from time to time – however well designed the resources are, students will need back-up for those times when they just can't 'get it' on their own.
- Provide a one-size-fits-all solution – differentiation needs to be built in (see Chapter 9).
- Completely replace books, handouts and other paper-based resources for the foreseeable future, since learners need variety in the ways in which material is presented to them.
- Replace the need for peer-to-peer communication and mutual support between learners, since it is so often fellow students who help to make learning happen – and indeed help us to make our teaching work.

Using online learning to stimulate campus-based students' learning

As suggested above, online learning works best when it integrates seamlessly into the overall learning experience. It is perfectly possible to bring interaction with teachers and fellow-learners into online learning but this must not just be an option to work well, it must be carefully nurtured and developed. The work of Gilly Salmon (2004) on e-moderating illustrates just how hard teachers need to work at stimulating communication between learners in virtual learning environments, and shows that when done well this can be very successful indeed with the virtual aspects of learning for college-based students every bit as productive as the traditional learning contexts.

Making teaching work now extends to making well-informed decisions about what exactly is best learned by students working alone with online technology, and what is best reserved for face-to-face interactive contexts, where tone of voice, body language and the opportunity for teachers to respond instantly to learners' puzzled expressions remain. If learners sitting on their own are puzzled by something it is all too easy for them to give up on it and move on to something else, but with the questions which puzzled them still unanswered.

Online learning for campus-based students works best when it feeds into all their other learning contexts. For example, preparation for a lecture can be done online, and follow-up activities can be done after the lecture and will feed into related tutorials and group exercises. But this requires teachers not just to *teach* in lectures, tutorials and so on, but to continuously link what learners are doing there into the other things that they are expected to be doing on their own in the virtual learning environment. In particular, it can be useful for teachers to explain which parts of the intended learning outcomes are being addressed in the face-to-face sessions, and which are being channelled through the virtual learning environment.

Online learning to enhance campus-based learning

As online learning becomes more sophisticated, it is apparent that such learning environments can provide excellent opportunities for learning. These include, for example:

- Online business simulations, where individuals and teams of students can work on real world problems with genuine data in a risk-free environment, for example with materials based on financial markets and using live data.
- Medical simulations, where health and allied professionals can experiment (for example with drug dosage on simulated patients) in ways that would not be feasible with live patients.
- Built-environment virtual site visits, since nowadays health and safety regulations make it nigh on impossible to get students on-site to really difficult or challenging building contexts.
- Online study-skills coaching, to replace or supplement classes given in college which are often attended by those who least need them. Students, particularly those from disadvantaged backgrounds, may be prepared to access such materials online whereas they may be unwilling to admit that they need face-to-face tuition on these matters.
- Online question-and-answer surgeries, which are more cost-effective and satisfactory than an endless line of individuals queuing at tutors' doors to ask very similar questions.

Putting the learning into online learning: developing 're-usable learning objects'

As discussed throughout this book, learning essentially happens through doing and feedback. One of the most promising trends in the development of online learning is the present focus on 'learning objects'. Wikipedia (accessed in December 2006) illustrates definitions of the term as follows:

- 'Any entity, digital or non-digital, that may be used for learning, education or training'.
- 'Any digital resource that can be reused to support learning'.
- 'Web-based interactive chunks of e-learning designed to explain a stand-alone learning objective'.

Essentially, a learning object is a small element of learning with its own intended learning outcomes and associated assessment built in, where the focus is on appropriate learning-by-doing with feedback provided as necessary. The idea is that each individual learning object is a self-sufficient element of learning and that an online learning programme can be built up by linking a series of learning objects, so that custom-built learning programmes can be designed to meet as exactly as possible the particular requirements of learners. This saves reinventing wheels, and allows individual learning objects to play their part in quite diverse overall online learning programmes, provided of course that they are well designed, fit for purpose and at the right level for the programme. Many reusable learning objects are published on the internet by individual providers, and a web search quickly shows the potential and diversity of such objects.

A key issue with designing learning objects is to develop ways of categorising and organising the learning objects that enable ready retrieval and usage. Various approaches to meta-tagging are being explored, to ensure that databases of learning objects are easy to use. The principal problem associated with metadata tagging is in achieving consensus on the key terms used as tags, since words can have multiple meanings in different contexts. The concept of reusable learning objects is very simple; after all, books are themselves reusable learning objects. However, the development and application of learning objects that can be tagged by content topic, level, difficulty, author, subject area and institutional origin are more complex.

Online learning using all the senses

Digital media developments have made it much easier to include in online learning materials audio and video, and in more advanced simulation programmes kinaesthetic participation by learners as well. With the use of headphones, media-rich online learning materials can be used effectively in learning resources centres, even when neighbouring learners are studying quite different things.

The use of video and audio together can bring to online learning the vital dimensions of facial expression, tone of voice, gesture and body language, all adding to opportunities for learners to make sense of what they are learning, as well as illustrating to learners live events such as industrial processes or interviews and discussions with experts or practitioners.

Care needs to be taken to avoid extended audio or video elements, however, as it becomes all too easy for learners to sit back and watch and listen, and then for their attention to fade. The principles of design of reusable learning objects come into play when designing or selecting short multimedia extracts, each of which needs to have its own clear purposes in the overall learning experience. In particular, each element of audio or video needs to be integrated with some decision making or evaluation by learners, with built-in feedback telling them whether they have successfully achieved what was intended with each media element.

Involving students in the development of online learning materials

Because many students are already digital natives, we should not underestimate the value of their potential contributions to the development and design of online learning materials. Students have often developed advanced skills at web searching, and a group of students can quickly track down relevant resources which can be built into both online learning programmes and into new reusable learning objects.

Students are also particularly good at designing the interactive elements which are so crucial for successful online learning, and can compose feedback responses (for example) to correct options and distractors in multiple-choice questions. Students who have just mastered a curriculum element often have clearly in their minds the questions and ambiguities which preceded their mastery, and can therefore design questions and activities which hit the real learning agenda – and often doing this much better than their teachers who may well have forgotten how the light first dawned when learning these elements themselves.

Online assessment – magic bullet or manacle?

Online assessment has become the biggest growth area associated with the use of information and communications technologies in post-compulsory education, and a web search for 'online assessment' yields an enormous collection of sources. For example, in the UK there are significant numbers of projects on web-based and computer-based assessment being undertaken by the 24 subject centres of the Higher Education Academy, and by several of the 74 Centres for Excellence for Teaching and Learning which have been established by the Higher Education Funding Council for England. Reasons for the spectacular growth in the use of online assessment include:

- Large class sizes making it increasingly difficult to continue the usage of traditional assessment methods.
- Online assessment which can deliver quick or instant feedback to students on their performance.
- Technology which can be used to manage the assessment process, tracking students' performance and creating mark lists, taking much of the drudgery out of the assessment process for staff.

In particular, structured formats such as multiple-choice questions are now widely used for online assessment, and expertise in designing tests and exams has developed widely. It is gradually becoming apparent that this expertise can only be gained by extensive trialling and piloting of test items until the tests perform reliably and validly. There is a steep learning curve to be ascended before it becomes cost-effective to replace traditional assessment instruments with online ones.

High hopes have been placed on the potential of online assessment to radically remove the drudgery from a teacher's role. Online electronic submissions have the power to:

- Significantly reduce the amount of plagiarism.
- Provide very rapid turnaround for feedback comments.
- Enable more detailed comments on students' work.

Developments in both Australia and the UK have harnessed the power of statement banks (see Brown et al., 1994) together with electronic in-text marking, to enable very rapid and detailed commentary to be returned to students. Statement banks essentially harness a repertoire of frequently used comments by an individual or group of assessors, which can effectively form a database of comments which can be used as necessary to produce an idiosyncratic commentary on an individual's work.

Innovations in automatic marking of free text have not been as successful as was originally hoped five years ago. However, more recently there have been exciting developments in the use of role-referencing grammar which are making this more likely.

In reviewing online assessment, it is easy to over-claim the benefits without taking full account of the complexity. As curriculum delivery declines in importance within the teacher's role in comparison with the roles of assessment and support, it has yet to be discovered to what extent the role of individualised commentary between tutors and students will continue to be valued. We believe that this role will continue to have importance for the foreseeable future, especially in the context of increased attention being paid to personalised learning at school.

What next in online learning?

Online learning is likely to mature quite rapidly as the next generation of digital natives takes over the design and implementation of the medium. In particular, online learning will become used much more wisely, and will no longer be seen as something which is suitable for all learning, but as a tool in the overall toolkit of teaching and learning approaches which can be chosen when it is really fit for the purposes of particular elements of learning. For example, typically podcasts use ten minute soundbytes rather than presenting lectures, and Gilly Salmon (2007) reports that some 50 per cent of students review the material again, for anything up to six times. So podcasts can be valuable for revision rather than necessarily first-level content delivery (namely, causing engagement and motivation rather than merely a substitution of the way in which course content is received by students).

Salmon (2007) also suggests that future e-developments will see significant enhancement in:

- the personalisation of learning (for just about all students nowadays have personal electronic devices of some kind);
- mobility (particularly the accessibility of material through podcasts);
- open source content (with institutions such as MIT and now the OU's 'Open Content' providing access to OU material to all for free);
- what many term 'Web 2.0' (that is the whole range of rich media used currently by our student generation for sharing knowledge, photos, video-streaming, profile-making, web-linked real physical spaces, syndication, material on the web readable by others) and similar.

The following interactive table is our attempt to chart the possible future of online learning – and you may well like to add your own views and experience where we have not attempted to make predictions (you need to remember, of course, how unwise it would have been twenty years ago to try to predict the state of online technology today in 2007!).

Development	*How likely is this?*	*How soon might this happen: your guess?*	*How useful will it be?*	*What might make it happen?*	*What might stop it?*
Every student in post-compulsory education will have online access, every-where, all the time.	Very likely that almost every student will have it most places most of the time. The final 5 per cent of students will be the toughest nut to crack.		Very: it will radically alter the entire nature of post-compulsory learning.	Government commitment to cheap or free ubiquitous broadband; ever cheaper and more portable hand-held devices; the will of teachers to make it happen.	Participant reluctance, particularly from students who are not digital natives.
Libraries containing paper-based resources will become redundant as students become able to access everything as digital resources.	Fairly likely, since digitalisation of resources is already proceeding apace.		Absolutely liberating for learners, although information literacy skills would then be even more important to enable students to locate relevant materials.	Buy-in by publishers, who need to become convinced that this will not destroy their markets. Reframing of information specialists' job descriptions. Rethinking of curriculum design and delivery by teachers.	Unsolvable copyright issues. Resistance by techno-Luddites.
Computer-based assessment of free text will be successful and ubiquitous.	Moderately likely. We already have successful assessment of word-strings in disciplines with strong factual content. Pioneering work on textual analysis including role-referencing grammar (see Guest, 2006) is making intelligent computer analysis of free text more likely.		Highly useful, since it could help to eliminate delays in giving feedback, and could maximise feed-forward.	Commitment by higher education institutions and researchers to solve some of the currently intractable problems associated with wide linguistic variation.	Resistance by some exam agencies and professional bodies. Some continuing intractable problems. The expense associated with complex research in this area.
Plagiarism will be entirely eliminated from online learning.	Unlikely, since every solution is likely to have a work-around which can be exploited by highly intelligent plagiarists.		Extremely, since this is currently a major concern associated with online learning.	A requirement that all work be submitted digitally and stored in-definitely so that new submissions can be checked against old. The further development of computer-based plagiarism detection services like Turnitin. Increasing digitisation of journals and other source materials.	Very determined plagiarists, including those who use ghost writers and impersonation.
Students will work together in cooperative learning teams without any necessity for teacher intervention.	Unlikely. We argue that tutor support is probably nowadays the most vital element supporting learning of all kinds.		Senior managers would be delighted because of the cost-effectiveness of the solutions. Students and tutors however might consider it less useful. Nevertheless, it's important to remember that peer-to-peer learning is increasingly recognised as a significant component of learning in the post-compulsory world.	The development of really excellent independent learning guides, including training not only in the use of content, but also in effective peer-support and learning.	Student and staff reluctance.
All teaching at post-compulsory level, everywhere in the world, would be in the medium of the English (American) language.	Quite likely. It is already very common for Scandinavian and continental undergraduate and postgraduate courses to be taught in English, and much online learning is also in English.		Very useful for English speakers, and for building world-wide communities of learners. However, since culture is so closely aligned to language, there would be significant detrimental aspects to this development.	Increasing use of English as a *lingua-franca*. Developments by large international publishers, with high market ambitions. The colonialisation of post-compulsory education by the English-speaking world.	Strong-minded national groups resisting this kind of linguistic colonisation of the intellectual world.

8

Managing assessment and feedback

This chapter addresses the following questions:

- What do we mean by assessment and feedback?
- Why are they so important in making teaching work?
- What has gone wrong with them, so that often they are not presently making teaching work?
- How best can we adjust them so they succeed in making teaching work with our students?

Smarter assessment and feedback

Designing assessment and giving students useful feedback on their learning are perhaps the most significant elements of the work of teachers in post-compulsory education. This is where the time is spent, and therefore much can be gained by making assessment and feedback smarter. Too often, in universities and colleges, assessment and feedback processes have changed too little, while student numbers have grown dramatically, and the pressures on teachers have increased accordingly. We simply can't do now for 250 students what we used to do (often successfully enough) for 25 students a few years ago. We need to rethink assessment and feedback, and we hope this chapter will help you to take steps to make these dimensions of your work smarter.

Assessment as a principal driver of learning

Race (2005) in his chapter entitled 'Assessment driving learning' puts the case that (after John Cowan) assessment is the engine which drives student learning, and that most students are (sensibly) quite strategic in their approaches to learning. Students devote energy to those aspects which count towards their final qualifications, often at the expense of other elements which could contribute significantly to their overall learning experience. In short, students get their heads down to learning when there is some assessed element involved. This means that teaching works best when it is seen by students to relate quite directly to their assessment. Even though 'teaching to the exam' is seen by most teachers in higher education to be undesirable, their students don't think so!

Therefore, it can be argued that to make teaching really work, we need to make systematic and thoughtful use of assessment as the principal driver of the learning of most of our students. However, although it may be assessment which causes students to get their heads down and do some learning, it is through the associated feedback that we can attempt to improve the nature and quality of that learning. In short, feedback can be the lubricant for the engine which drives student learning.

Research has shown (see for example Yorke, 2002) that assessment and feedback are strongly linked to student retention. When students receive early feedback on their progress in a course or module, they are less likely to end up dropping out of higher education. Assessment and associated feedback are key factors impacting on student motivation and commitment.

The UK's National Student Survey

This was set up as a result of the UK government's White Paper 'The Future of Higher Education' (DfES, 2003), where it was decided that the National Union of Students should compile data about the quality of the student experience in higher education, to enable applicants for places to make informed decisions about the quality they would be able to expect from different institutions in each major subject's discipline area. The survey was first run in England and Wales in 2005, then extended to Scotland in 2006. Final year students were asked to indicate their satisfaction levels against statements relating to 21 aspects of their experience of higher education, and five of these statements addressed assessment and feedback. In both years (to date), students' experience of assessment and feedback has been the least satisfactory of all the areas of experience surveyed.

The five statements relating to assessment and feedback are as follows:

- The *criteria* used in marking have been clear in advance.
- Assessment arrangements and marking have been *fair*.
- Feedback on my work has been *prompt*.

- I have received *detailed* comments on my work.
- Feedback on my work has helped me clarify things I did not *understand*. (our italics)

We will return with some practical suggestions relating to these aspects of assessment and feedback in Chapter 10, but meanwhile it can be argued that the first two aspects here are less of a problem than the other three. Criteria are usually quite clear in advance, but are often hidden away in course or module handbooks, or on intranet files. All that is really needed is for teachers to bring them more overtly to the attention of students in lectures and tutorials, explaining what the criteria actually mean in practice. It is also helpful to link them more firmly to the sorts of evidence which students are expected to deliver to demonstrate that they have achieved the intended learning outcomes to the levels indicated by the assessment criteria.

Similarly, considerable care and attention are invested in assessment and marking arrangements being fair, but not enough energy is devoted to explaining to students how, exactly, this is achieved. We need to let students know about the care that is taken in designing exam questions, for example, and in moderating the standard of marking of their exam answers. You could also explain the vital role that is played by external examiners in ensuring that the arrangements are indeed fair.

However, issues remain regarding feedback. Students say that it is not prompt enough, nor do they feel they have received sufficiently detailed comments on their work, and that the feedback they receive does not help them enough in clarifying things which they did not understand. Clearly there remains a case for us to smarten up our thinking about how and when we give our students feedback, not least as this is an aspect of our job which already takes up a great deal of our time and energy in any case.

What's wrong with assessment?

At an international conference on assessment, as part of a symposium about 'Changing hearts regarding assessment', participants were asked to write on Post-its their heartfelt completions of the following sentence: 'Assessment would be better at making learning happen with my students if only … '. The table below represents their thoughts about what we need to do (and what students need to do) to make assessment a better driver for learning. There is, of course, some overlap, but it is interesting to see where the overlaps lie – signposting the most serious of the problems we face in trying to make assessment fit for purpose.

Assessment would be better at making learning happen with my students if only ...

- I had more time to spend having individual assessments that truly met their personal learning requirements.
- We could forget percentage marks and leave just feedback and pass/fail/merit instead.
- I could spend more time on assessment and less on delivery.
- We did not have grades at final level undergraduate study.
- They realised the importance of the process to their future development.
- There were less dilemmas and constraints in the assessment process.
- They didn't wait till the last minute to do any work.
- They knew what is expected and they could steer themselves there with some guidance from me.
- I had more time with individuals or groups rather than 200 at a time.
- I spent more time on working with others on preparing them for assessment.
- I could talk through drafts with them as part of the learning process, in a detailed manner.
- We introduced a systematic regime of formative assessment.
- They found a self-fulfillment value in the assessment.
- The university would not impose dead criteria based on what is easy to measure rather than what we want students to do.
- The assessment criteria were transparent and understandable.
- They would recognise that I am not assessing them, their worth, but their ideas.
- It was more person-centred (individual, applicable) to the students.
- We took into account their individual learning needs.
- Both the students and myself could negotiate and discuss what matters in their learning.
- Students themselves were more involved in the design of the assessment.
- Feed-forward was more constructive across the board.
- It was a true reflection of their work.
- We got the students to evaluate the success and impact of the chosen assessment process on their learning.
- They were less anxious about it.
- All colleagues would take the time to think more about learning and assessment.
- They were aware of how and why it is done.
- It involved self-assessment.
- The feedback could be oral and one-to-one (for hundreds of students!).
- I was free to choose the most appropriate assessment.
- There weren't so many students!
- The overall module design allowed feedback to influence future learning.
- All lecturers adopted similar principles relating to support and feed-forward – especially in the early stages.
- It were more fun and more enjoyable.
- My students understood the value of it in affecting their learning.
- Course texts were more accessible in terms of language difficulty.
- The system was more flexible – we are chained to percentages.
- The learning outcomes were transparent to the students.
- I would make the purpose clear and give clear instruction to the students about what they ought to do.
- They truly valued the process and afforded the optimum amount of time needed for it.
- It valued the students' active involvement in the process – peer- and self-assessment are known to have benefits, but not used enough!
- I really knew what I was doing – and they really knew what they were doing.

Perhaps the last of these quotations sums it up (*if only* – 'I really knew what I was doing – and they really knew what they were doing')? But there are some notable trends in the responses of these delegates, including:

- Assessment is not yet playing an optimum part in making teaching work.
- Many teachers in higher education feel constrained by the systems in which they are implementing assessment, not least the requirement to use percentage scores.
- Colleagues often feel that they are 'out on a limb' in their approaches to assessment, and wish that other colleagues viewed assessment in similar ways.
- Many practitioners see value in using self- and peer-assessment, and wish that students were more often involved in the design and implementation of assessment.

The participants at this particular conference were largely a self-selecting group of practitioners who know already a great deal about assessment, and care a lot about making it work well – often fighting battles in their own institutions to improve assessment processes, practices and instruments. In other words, they are in a position to be expert witnesses regarding the problems encountered in the context of assessment.

Towards fit for purpose assessment

Among the reasons for assessment and feedback being found by students to be the least satisfactory elements of their experience of higher education is the fact that too often assessment is not 'fit for purpose'. Too often, the actual assessment processes and instruments which we use cannot be considered the most sensible ways to measure students' achievement of the intended learning outcomes of their programmes. Too often, historical precedents continue to influence our design of assessment. For example time-constrained, unseen, written examinations only manage to measure a shadow of students' actual learning, as filtered through their pen-and-paper communication in exam rooms. Students themselves are now much more familiar with keyboards and web-searches, and writing with pen on paper 'from memory' is a quite an alien domain. To assess 'smarter', we need to go back to the intended learning outcomes of our programmes, and decide what sorts of evidence of achievement most closely link to the demonstration of successful achievement of these outcomes. We need to be quite selective as to which aspects of this evidence can be successfully demonstrated with pen and paper in exam rooms. We need also to decide how best to use formative feedback to assist students in their journey towards demonstrating their level of achievement of the intended learning outcomes.

Attention to five aspects of our design of assessment and feedback can help us on our journey towards making teaching work: vailidity, reliability, transparency, authenticity, and manageability.

Validity

This is about to what extent we are actually measuring, with our assessment processes and instruments, exactly what we are intending to measure – students' demonstrated evidence of achievement of the intended learning outcomes. If we are merely measuring what students can remember in exam rooms about what they have been taught, we should worry that we're not assessing smartly. We often need to step back, and ask ourselves how best we can attempt to measure student learning, without the undue influence of such factors as pen-and-paper filters under exam conditions. In many parts of the world, it is already well known that face-to-face, question-and-answer interrogations come closer to finding out to what extent students have got their heads around the principles of a subject. Perhaps in the UK (for example), we're too hung up on precedents and place too much trust in the validity of exams, and over-use this form of assessment in higher education simply because it has become an acceptable way of assessing students' knowledge and skills.

Reliability

We need to be accountable with our assessment. It has got to be seen by all as being fair and consistent. If we just make subjective judgements on the evidence students give us of their level of achievement of the intended learning outcomes, we're in trouble. Students might appeal against our assessment decisions. Not long ago this would have been unheard of. But now that students see themselves much more as consumers of higher education, if they feel that they have not been treated fairly they will complain, and their complaints may reach a court of law. Therefore, part of assessing smarter is to make sure that we've already constructed a robust framework to defend, where needed, our assessment decisions. In short, we need to be able to prove beyond all reasonable doubt that our assessment verdicts can be upheld, and that they are firmly linked to the published criteria which we can relate to the quality and nature of students' evidence of achievement of our intended learning outcomes.

Transparency

Partly as a consequence of widening participation policies, where there are now many students in post-compulsory education from backgrounds where there is no familiarity with how such higher levels of education actually work, it has become increasingly important that assessment in particular is made transparent to our students. We now need to make it abundantly clear to them exactly what our standards are, and what we expect them to demonstrate to achieve their awards.

By far the most effective way to achieve transparency is through formative feedback to students long before such critical assessment elements as final exams. We should reveal to students the fine details of our actual expectations and help them towards becoming better able to provide evidence of their achievement. In other words, an increasingly important aspect of feedback to students on their work is the dimension of helping them to tune in to the assessment culture in which they are participating.

Authenticity

At least some of the reforms to assessment in post-compulsory education in recent years are in the direction of making sudden-death examinations less significant, and taking more account of ongoing performance in coursework along the way towards awards. However, plagiarism has become ever more of a problem, and coursework elements are beset by the possibility of students using other people's work inappropriately. This has increased the need to be able to be seen to be able to guarantee the authenticity of students' coursework products. Plagiarism detection software plays a significant part as a deterrent against inappropriate use of others' work by students, but prevention of plagiarism is preferable to detection and subsequent punishment or disqualification.

In practice, plagiarism is much more easily recognised in face-to-face contexts, for example when students are quizzed – even very briefly – on their work. It only takes a few well-directed questions about a piece of coursework to give indications about the level of authenticity behind that work.

Manageability

This is the dimension of assessment and feedback which has quite rapidly gone out of control. Attempting to carry out with 250 students the same sorts of assessment and feedback which once worked perfectly well with 25 students soon becomes quite unmanageable. That is why we now need to design assessment and feedback more smartly. If our lives are taken up with the increased burden of assessing more and more students and giving them feedback, the quality of both processes suffers, and we have too little time and energy left to ensure that our assessment is valid, reliable, authentic and transparent, or that our feedback is timely, useful, and promotes learning.

The need to diversify assessment

In past times when only a relatively small proportion of the population participated in post-compulsory education, it seemed acceptable to use a quite restricted range of assessment processes and instruments, and exams, essays and reports formed the bulk of the assessment culture. Now that around half of the population is expected to experience post-compulsory education, things have changed. Every assessment format disadvantages some students, so we need to extend and diversify the range of assessment processes and instruments that we use, so that fewer students are repeatedly disadvantaged by over-used formats. Making teaching work is very much about making assessment work, and the latter is best achieved by diversifying the range and scope of the instruments and processes we use to measure and accredit students' achievement.

In relatively recent history, many study programmes were assessed primarily by end-of-course exams, with the assessment of coursework playing a relatively insignificant role. It can be argued that this resulted in an 'examinocracy', with those students who developed good exam skills succeeding, to the detriment of other students whose learning was equally successful, but who were not so good at demonstrating their achievement through the medium of exams. With widening participation, this anomaly has to be addressed and compensation made, so that the success of learning is accredited with much less dependence on the particular means of measurement and accreditation.

Smarter assessment, therefore, needs to include appropriate diversification of the assessment agenda, to ensure that all students have the opportunity to demonstrate their achievement in ways which they are comfortable with, rather than in a few prescribed ways.

Feedback and feed-forward

As illustrated by the National Student Survey in the UK, feedback is often an area where students feel that our teaching is not working well. Too often, feedback focuses on failings rather than achievements, and saps students' confidence levels. In particular, students need help when getting feedback on their work, so that they can address deficiencies and improve their next element of assessed work; the forward-pointing aspects of feedback are often referred to as 'feed-forward'.

When there were small numbers in classes, traditional methods of giving feedback – such as writing comments onto their work – were effective enough, but now that student cohorts often number several hundred, this is no longer efficient enough to work well for students. The feedback can be too late for them to act on it, and the task of writing comments on hundreds of essays or reports is so daunting and time-consuming that the level of helpfulness of the comments decreases dramatically.

Nowadays, however, technology can come to our rescue regarding feedback. For example, we can send feedback by email, and use word-processing tools to compose individual feedback emails from a collection of frequently-needed explanations and comments. This means that students still get their feedback individually, and at a time and place where they have the relative comfort of privacy to reflect on it, rather than in the more stressful face-to-face situation where they feel that we may be watching their reactions to our feedback.

Race (2005), in staff development workshops on 'Smarter Feedback', asked participants from a wide range of institutions (and in several countries) to perform a group task where they wrote all the different methods whereby their students received feedback on separate Post-its, and then placed them on a chart where the horizontal axis represented 'efficiency for staff' and the vertical axis represented 'learning pay-off for students'.

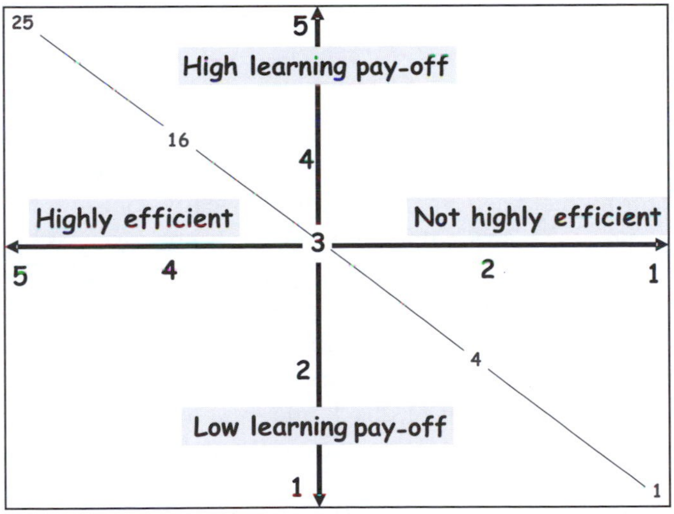

Figure 8.1 Feedback to students: learning pay-off versus efficiency for staff (Source: Race, 2005)

Workshop participants were then asked to score the efficiency and learning pay-off for each feedback process, and multiply the two scores to give a relative estimate of the value of each process. Trends which emerged from such workshops are summarised by the following list:

High scoring feedback methods:
25 learners self-assessing
25 learners cross-marking
25 peer-marking with feedback
25 feedback from patients and clients
25 emails to group
25 peer-assessment
20 peer feedback
20 constructive questioning within groups
20 self-evaluation
20 verbal feedback to whole class
20 emailing with attachments

Low scoring feedback methods:
5 no feedback at all
5 one-to-one verbal feedback
4 internal test with grading and feedback
4 written feedback that isn't read
4 grades with oral correction
4 written exams
3 individual written comments on work
3 web conferencing
3 written assignment feedback sheets
1 marks or grades without comments

Notice that 'no feedback at all' scores '5' here – '1' for zero learning pay-off multiplied by '5' for high efficiency! This means that many common feedback methods are *worse* than no feedback at all, if we multiply effectiveness by efficiency in this way! Note also that the high-scoring processes include 'feedback from patients and clients' as reported by a group of medical educators, who explained that their students took much more notice of such feedback, and that it was extremely efficient for the educators as they were not doing it themselves. A further trend is the value of peer feedback and peer-assessment processes, where again it can be argued that the efficiency from the staff point of view is very high, and the pay-off from the student point of view is also high, as students learn at least as much through the processes of judging others' work and giving feedback as well as by receiving it from their peers.

Do students take notice of our feedback?

Too often, the answer is "No!" Many assessors bemoan the fact that they are left with uncollected essays, assignments and reports, all containing feedback which is never going to be seen by the intended recipients. This is often because the marked work only becomes available such a long time after the students have worked on it that they no longer care about it, and have moved on to other modules. Sometimes the only thing that students took any notice of was a score or a grade. Even any well-intentioned feed-forward was completely wasted. Feedback is much more likely to be heeded if it is received quickly. But what can we do to achieve this?

Getting feedback to students within 24 hours

It is widely accepted that feedback on students' work works best when it is received quickly, while they still remember clearly what they were trying to do in their efforts. In Australia the work of Sadler (1989, 1998, 2003) has consistently emphasised the role of formative feedback in leading students towards successful learning. Gibbs and Simpson (2002) looked critically at the decline in the quantity and quality of formative feedback which students receive as class sizes grow in a climate of policies about widening participation in higher education. Bowl (2003) provides a wealth of detail about how students react to feedback (or the lack of it) in her book based on interviews with non-traditional entrants to higher education. Yorke (2002) writes convincingly of the role (and speed) of formative feedback in addressing student non-completion, and Knight and Yorke (2003) continue the argument that there are major problems in higher education with assessment and formative feedback, an argument developed further by Race (2005).

Some feedback can be nearly instantaneous, for example when using computer-based or online multiple-choice exercises, where the feedback to choosing distractors (or correct options) can appear on-screen as soon as students select an option. Salmon (2004) illustrates the power of well-moderated online feedback to students, and discusses in detail what can be done to make online learning a productive and active learning experience.

However, it is often the case that students get feedback on essays, reports and problems-sheets, much too late – it can take weeks to mark their work, particularly if the class size is large. By the time students receive their feedback they may well have moved on, and then they take very little notice of that feedback. Colleagues in many institutions complain that too many students don't even bother to pick up their marked work. Even when much care, effort and time have been put into writing the feedback, it often ends up entirely wasted! Life is too short to waste time on composing feedback that won't be read or used.

Feedback (on paper, and face-to-face with whole groups) can often be given to students within 24 hours of them engaging with the work they hand in for assessment. Consider the following ...

1 Suppose that students are asked to bring their completed assignment (essay, report, whatever) to a whole-class session, for example a lecture – say the 10–11 a.m. lecture next Tuesday morning.
2 Advise them that the deadline for receipt of their work is 10 a.m. on Tuesday morning, and the (only) place they can hand in that assignment is at the lecture during the first minute or two.
3 Ask all the students to place their work in a pile on the lecture bench, in the first two minutes of the lecture period. By 10:02 a.m. or so, you have all their work (and a good attendance).
4 As soon as you've got all of their work (for example 10:03), hand out to the group a pre-prepared feedback sheet on the assignment concerned – on a coloured sheet of paper (different colours for successive assignments) so that you can easily refer to the sheet. This feedback sheet can contain:
   - explanations to anticipated, frequently-occurring problems;
   - illustrations of components of a good answer to the assignment question;
   - examples of useful source materials and references;
   - model solutions of quantitative parts of the assignment (if applicable);
   - and so on. It is useful for you to number the paragraphs on this coloured feedback sheet, to make it easier for you to refer to its contents later.
5 Allow your class two or three minutes to scan through the feedback sheet (for example 10:03–10:06).
6 Next (say 10:06–10:09), talk the whole group through one or two of the most significant of the feedback areas on the sheet, adding tone-of-voice, body language and eye contact to help the meaning of your feedback to be really clear to the students, augmenting one or two of the paragraphs on your feedback sheet.
7 Then proceed with the lecture as normal.
8 When you proceed to mark their work, you've now no need to write the same things on so many different assignments, and can make your feedback much more specific and individual to each student regarding his/her triumphs and disasters. This means that when they get your feedback, they pay much more attention to it.

Most of the students will still have been finishing off the assignment – or at least giving it a final check, *within the last 24 hours*. This means they are now getting feedback while they still have a very clear view on what they were trying to do in the assignment, and can remember what their difficulties may have been. They are therefore getting a lot of feedback while they really *want* to know how their work will fare in assessment – they are thirsty for feedback at this point. Some students may indeed have only *started* on the assignment during the last 24 hours – these are likely to be the ones who need the feedback the most, and they are very receptive to it at this time.

How this feedback method saves you a lot of time!

When you actually go away to mark your students' work, you can save up to two-thirds of the time you would normally have spent marking it. You save time and energy as follows:

- You don't have to write the same things on many different students' assignments – the common mistakes and difficulties have already been covered by your feedback sheet, and you can simply write 'Please see Point 5 on the green sheet' and so on.
- Because you've debriefed your students *orally* in the whole group about the most important points in your pre-prepared feedback, there's little need to mention these points in any additional feedback you write on their assignments, other than to sometimes remind them of your oral debriefing.
- If you've included the process of asking students to self-assess their work, based on your generic and specific feedback, you can be sure that they have reflected on their work and on your feedback in ways which deepen their learning, making the time and energy you have devoted to providing both episodes of feedback all the more worthwhile.
- Your growing collection of feedback sheets will continue to be available as evidence of your good teaching practices, and can be included in submissions to external examiners, professional bodies, and in your appraisal or review documentation.

There are, however, at least three questions which spring up in the minds of many colleagues confronted with the above suggestions on giving students feedback at the moment of submission of their work.

1 *"But what about students who don't hand it in on time?"* There are no extensions! The real world works to deadlines – for funding bids, conference contributions, job interviews, and so on. It's good to train students to meet deadlines. Anyone who misses the deadline is not, however, completely stuffed. They have the opportunity to do 'Alternative Assignment B' which addresses the same learning outcomes as the original, but where the coloured feedback sheet is of no help. They can hand the alternative assignment in for another deadline. (There are subtle ways of making Alternative Assignment B somehow less attractive than the original assignment!)
2 *"If the feedback on the coloured sheet is so valuable, why can't we give out this guidance in advance of students doing the assignment?"* We can give out the guidance in advance – but it doesn't work! When students have detailed guidance, many of them will read it, but will soon get so busy doing the assignment that they

will ignore or forget most of the guidance, and still get into the (anticipated) difficulties that the coloured feedback sheet addresses. Feedback only really seems to work *after* students have done something.

3 *"Won't many of the students find it very stressful, getting so much feedback on what may be wrong with their work so quickly?"* The answer to this question is "Yes", but we can do a lot to dissipate this stress. For example, a couple of minutes into our explanations of the key difficulties which students may have encountered, we can ask for a show of hands in response to a question such as "How many of you now realise that you had trouble with this particular point in your own work?" When many hands are raised, students can see that they are by no means alone and will take at least some comfort in that the difficulties were relatively common to many in the room.

Giving students feedback, and getting them to work out their marks

An extension of the above idea is to return students' marked work to them (after giving generic feedback as described above, and now containing specific individual feedback) *without* their marks. Gibbs and Simpson (2002) and others have commented on the negative affects associated with giving students their marks and feedback at the same time – students are blinded by the marks, and the value of the feedback is eclipsed (Race, 2005). In this case let students *use* the individual feedback on their work, and the generic feedback already received, to work out their marks for themselves. Race (2006) suggests that if the students' self-assessment is within 5 per cent or one grade point of the tutor-assessed mark, let the higher number go forward.

Conclusion

We hope that you have gained useful ideas from this chapter, to help you use assessment and feedback to make your teaching work. It is, however, quite difficult to change assessment and feedback systems, which are often embedded deeply into the way institutions and departments manage assessment and feedback. If it were easy to improve these systems, it can be argued that it would already have been done long ago. That said, the more we know about what exactly the problems are with assessment and feedback, the better we can go about changing obsolete systems, so that assessment and feedback can be useful tools in teaching and learning, rather than barriers and obstacles.

9

Differentiation

This chapter addresses the following questions:

- How can we effectively design a curriculum that enables differentiation?
- How can we ensure delivery efficiently supports different learning needs?
- How can we design assessment to accurately differentiate student performance?

Introduction

Widening participation has resulted in some higher education programmes attracting a variety of students from diverse academic backgrounds with a wide range of student abilities, interests and reasons for following the programme. It is not unknown for large, mixed ability cohorts with differing attainment levels and expectations to follow a shared curriculum in the first, and sometimes even in the second, year of a programme. The changing student:staff ratios in higher education mean that sometimes foundation, undergraduate and even postgraduate students are taught together. In these cases all students may experience the same learning activities irrespective of the programme chosen or academic background.

At the same time there are many pressures on staff to focus their efforts on equal opportunity and inclusivity. In order to ensure that all students on a programme are able to participate, it is often easiest for staff simply to remove challenging or difficult aspects from the learning experience. This pressure can in practice manifest itself in restricted opportunities, in particular for more able students.

The mixed-ability learning environment has implications for student learning and brings with it challenges for us in supporting individual students to reach their individual potential. One implication of mixed ability cohorts and inclusivity is that we need to consider carefully how to efficiently differentiate the experience and performance of the range of students without disadvantaging particular groups of students. Teaching mixed groups of students together may not provide any of them with a suitably intellectually challenging environment and whilst it is prudent to ask whether the course is appropriate for all students taking it, it falls to you to accommodate the range of student abilities and interests.

Why is differentiation important?

Clearly we have a responsibility to be able to differentiate strong performances from weaker performances of graduating students. However, it is perhaps even more important that students are given appropriate opportunities throughout their programme to develop their potential. Many students, demotivated by an ill-fitting course, focus solely on the need to complete assessment tasks, and resort to surface and strategic learning. If we can efficiently and effectively ensure that content is interesting, tasks are stretching without being threatening, and delivery methods are suited to individual need, then students are more likely to engage in deep and meaningful learning.

How may we differentiate?

In order to effectively differentiate the individual student learning experience we need to be able to offer a variety of opportunities and assess a broad spectrum of achievement. Less able students need to be supported to achieve and more able students should have the scope to work beyond the curriculum.

When considering differentiation of student performance it is natural to turn to assessment design and indeed all differentiation of learning begins with student assessment. However, there is little point focusing solely on assessment as it will be necessary to align both curriculum and delivery methods to successfully support changes in assessment. It's necessary to consider what you can do in all aspects of your dealings with students in order to encourage each to reach their potential. It is useful to ask yourself the following questions about your students:

- What type of people are they?
- What previous knowledge and experience do they have?
- What do they want to achieve from the programme?
- What do they need to learn from the programme?
- What obstacles do they face?
- Why are they following the programme?

Differentiated curriculum

Given that you are likely to be faced with a wide range of interests and abilities in any given class does it make sense to offer a common curriculum?

Clearly you have to be pragmatic here. It is not realistic to be able to offer completely different curricula to different students (nor in many cases desirable) but if you reflect you may find that you are already currently investing considerable time and effort in trying to support students who are struggling with the curriculum, motivating students who are not interested in the curriculum and trying to excite students unchallenged by the curriculum. If you invest the time you currently spend on supporting students following ill-fitting curricula in designing more appropriate curricula, then this may reap benefits. By front loading our efforts, we may improve both efficiency and effectiveness.

However, if you are to offer a differentiated curriculum it is important that you explain the rationale to students and ensure that you clarify the concept of fairness. Establish the fact that each student is a unique individual with different learning needs. Better still, actively involve each student in designing their own curriculum. So how can you go some way to ensuring students are following suitable and differentiated curricula?

Differentiation through ability grouping (streaming)

There is a wealth of information about the positive effects of ability grouping in secondary education. It seems logical, given the increased population moving into higher education that higher education establishments should consider following suit.

It is common in higher education to group students for pragmatic reasons and because it is widely recognised that group working skills are desirable in graduates, yet it is not the norm in higher education to stream students into ability groupings within programmes. We tend not to group by ability (or learning style, or even by interest) but to group students whose ability may vary considerably. Curriculum polarisation through ability grouping is contentious because students can be disadvantaged by the limits placed on their work pace and attainment. Low ability groups are not provided with equal opportunities for achievement as high ability groups, and at the other end of the spectrum some students taught in high ability groups, faced with high expectations and fast-pace delivery, may resort to surface learning.

However, if we accept that students have innate differences in ability then their learning experience should take these differences into account. It makes sense to create homogeneous learning groups which allow you to provide an optimal level of study for the whole group. Students should be able to benefit not only from studying at a suitable pace but also from the mutual support and cooperation of their peers.

Those who argue against ability groupings often do so because they believe that all students should have equal opportunities. However, this is missing the point. Equal opportunity should not equate to identical experience but to the right of every student to learn. Talented students in mixed ability groupings are often disadvantaged by the students in their cohort. We need to give them the opportunity to benefit from working with intellectual peers and to experience an intellectually challenging environment which consistently meets their needs.

Ability grouping is controversial as it highlights individual differences in student ability, but if we are to provide a learning environment that meets the needs of students of all levels of ability we should consider this as an option. One approach to streaming students efficiently is to:

- Use regular formative assessment to determine individual student ability.
- Flexibly assign students who are struggling to groups which are working on less complex tasks than those attempted by more advanced students.
- Consider varying the level of task and requisite thinking skills between groups.
- Consider if it is more appropriate to give students the same task but to vary the level of outcome expected from each group of students.
- Use formative assessment of student progress to inform and permit movement between groups.

To assign students flexibly to groups on a module-by-module basis, according to their current levels of performance, need not necessarily bring with it significant overheads in terms of organisation, and it allows students to be appropriately challenged. As student learning will progress at different rates, you need to allow movement between groups and it should be feasible, using formative assessment, to respond to changes in students' achievement, needs and motivation by group reassignment as students develop.

Differentiation through involving students in research

Independent study through research projects allows you to vary the degree of support depending on an individual student's abilities and it is therefore worth considering to what extent it is feasible to allow students to take ownership of the curriculum. One way to engage stronger students may be to allow students' research to take them beyond the curriculum rather that limiting student learning by pre-specifying learning outcomes. Handled with care there is significant potential to make teaching work by involving students as partners in research. Through research, student ideas and knowledge can progress and move forward and students may enjoy sharing in the excitement of discovery, perceiving that they are working at the cutting edge of their subject. Managed correctly, student research can also offer efficiency gains if the outputs of research are used to inform the curriculum.

Differentiated delivery

Delivery in higher education has traditionally been primarily through large lectures. Lecturers understandably use a few students in the lecture hall as reference points for determining pace of delivery. As a result some students in mixed ability classes have to wait for the rest of the class to catch up, whilst others struggle to keep up with the pace. This mode of delivery will be alien to many first year students and they will adapt at different rates. Where you know the students in a lecture, you can try to direct higher level questions to those who can handle them and lower level questions to students with greater needs. By targeting questions towards students' abilities you can engage all students in thinking. However, realistically it is difficult to differentiate delivery in a large lecture and there are alternative modes of delivery which lend themselves much more to differentiated and even individualised delivery.

Differentiation using technological and other resources

We should be looking to provide alternative activities for the student who has already mastered curriculum content and to accelerate or decelerate the pace that students move through the curriculum depending upon their level of competence. Integration of technology can be a valuable tool in differentiating delivery based on individual student needs. There is a wealth of material available to students in learning centres, through learning resource materials and on the internet and as a result the requirement for you to deliver material is far reduced from even ten years ago. Identify a set of useful resources, activities and websites that are valuable and which a student can explore at any time. This will facilitate students working at their own pace and allow you to better focus your attentions. Consider your role. Perhaps you can spend less time on delivery to the whole cohort – direct them to where material can be found and focus your attentions instead on more bespoke, student-centred tutoring. If you exploit the potential of resources this can free up your time to address individual students' particular problems.

Differentiated assessment

It is accepted practice to give students a common assignment with a common deadline and to offer identical support to all students. This programme-centred rather than student-centred approach is born out of tradition and out of a need on the part of staff to manage the programme, within the restrictions set by external moderators and internal standards and with the restricted resources available to them. Faced with ever-increasing cohort sizes it is difficult for staff to find the time to focus on individual student learning needs and to offer appropriate support for individual students through the assessment process.

As a result staff often find themselves struggling to design assessments that will engage both the weakest and strongest students, and the resulting ill-fitting assessments may be a contributory factor to the rise in plagiarism that is being witnessed on many programmes.

It is efficient, both in terms of staff time and student learning, to address issues of differentiation at the assessment design stage rather than to offer ad hoc support or further opportunities as the need arises. It is considered good practice, with benefits for both students and staff, to align assessment and assessment criteria with learning outcomes. However, in some cases this practice may result in a formulaic 'painting by numbers' approach to assessment and you need to consider whether you are giving students enough scope both when you are specifying learning outcomes and also when you are relating your assessments to these learning outcomes.

Specification of learning outcomes

The common practice of specifying the higher education curriculum in terms of learning outcomes may have the effect of limiting learning. Knight and Yorke (2003) argue that designing curricula around explicit learning outcomes risks the inadvertent building-in of limitations on what strategic students need to do. Atherton (2002) goes one step further, suggesting that specifying learning outcomes is actually teacher-centric. By imposing on students the teacher's assumptions about what they will have learned at the end of a module or programme, we put students 'in an excessively and counter-productively dependent situation' (Atherton, 2002). Learning outcomes drive assessment and assessment drives student behaviour and so you need to think carefully when specifying learning outcomes about the implications for student behaviour.

- How will students evidence that they have met the learning outcome? Are you going to dictate this or will you allow students to choose how they will evidence learning? Consider the advantages of both approaches.
- How will you assess or measure whether a learning outcome has been met? There is little point in specifying a learning outcome that cannot be assessed. Equally, you need to honestly assess whether a particular learning outcome has been specified, primarily because it is easy to measure rather than because it contributes meaningfully to the student learning experience.
- How easy will it be for you to differentiate student performance against the

learning outcome? If it is not clear how this can be done then you may need to reconsider how the learning outcome is expressed. In many cases students can get through their courses by doing only what is required, namely, assessed. Students may strategically adopt surface learning in response to a teaching environment which fails to encourage them to adopt a deep approach.

Poorly considered learning outcomes can lead to the specification of tasks and activities that students see as pointless (and which often are!). If students do not see a connection between what they are being asked to do and their motivation for learning, they are unlikely to engage in deep learning. You need to ensure that you are not specifying learning outcomes that are too prescriptive and low level, and that you are offering scope and opportunity rather than limiting the learning of more able students.

Flexible assessment

Ideally, in many cases, assessment could be more focused around the individual. Students could become involved in negotiating aspects of their assessment such as:

- timing of the assessment;
- method of assessment;
- task;
- type of support given;
- how the piece of work will be marked and by whom.

By students taking more ownership of their assessments they take more responsibility for their learning, and it is possible to differentiate the student learning experience in the most direct and most effective way. However, with practicality, flexible assessment brings with it a plethora of related issues that need to be addressed for it to be effective. Firstly, you need to be confident that the assessment will evidence the required learning outcomes appropriately. You could give students the responsibility for identifying how learning outcomes are being met. If they are able to do this then this may be the most efficient approach, whilst at the same time developing students' independent learning and reflective abilities. Another related challenge is to ensure that students understand exactly what is being assessed and what they need to do to pass. Your role becomes one primarily of facilitator and mentor, ensuring that students are progressing towards a clearly agreed goal. You should consider using formative assessment to give students useful feedback during learning. Of equal importance is consideration of alignment of teaching and learning activities with the assessment. Where a common assessment is being used for all students in a cohort it is relatively straight forward to design appropriate and complementary materials, exercises and timetables. Where each student is working on a unique assignment, however, considerable care needs to be taken to ensure appropriate, effective and timely support is available to prepare students for the assessment.

In addition to all of these issues, you also need to consider how you will ensure fairness across assessments and how you will create a marking scheme to encompass a range of assignments. Also, you will need to be clear as to how you will reassess students if necessary. Finally, you need to check your internal quality assurance mechanisms to ensure that they currently allow negotiated assessment and that you will be able to meet validation processes, Quality Assurance Agency for Higher Education (QAA) specifications, benchmarks and requirements by professional bodies.

Given all these potential complications it is unsurprising that most lecturers choose not to move too far into the realms of flexible or student-centred assessment. However, this is a pity because most of these related issues can be addressed with solid planning and clear communication between tutors and students.

A sensible way to approach differentiation through flexible assessment is to introduce only those elements of flexibility or negotiation that will result in little or no overheads in terms of your time. You could consider:

- Giving students a list of assignment formats from which to choose, for example oral presentation, written report, demonstration, visual model. Initially there will be some outlay in terms of designing the assessments, but marking may be far less tedious and students can focus their efforts on creating something that interests them.
- Encouraging students to choose the aspects or the topic upon which they wish to report. Negotiate their choice with them. If all students are applying their knowledge to a different client area or topic then plagiarism may be reduced, students can make the assignment more relevant to their lives and, again, marking should be more interesting for you.
- Allowing students to identify which evidence they wish to put forward in portfolios to demonstrate their competency. This will develop students' core skills and enable students to individualise their portfolios.
- Allowing students to negotiate the assessment timings and submission date within limits and the type, frequency and quantity of formative and summative feedback they would like. When you consider how much effort you put into providing detailed written summative feedback that is never collected or used, doesn't it make sense to ask students if they would like this? You could also ask students to identify which areas they would like formative feedback to address.

Graduated assessment

Just as a commitment to equal opportunity should recognise the right of every student to learn, so it should recognise the need for every student to be challenged by assessment. Good assessment design should offer challenges to students of all abilities. It is often useful to scaffold an assessment brief, particularly for first year students, in order to identify the amount of marks available for each aspect or part of the assignment. A good assignment brief will allocate 40 per cent of the marks (or whatever is regarded as a minimal pass mark) to an element that requires significant effort on the part of the student but does not require processing at the highest cognitive levels. Marks above this should be allocated for elements requiring higher level skills, becoming exponentially more difficult. These 'sting in the tail' assignments involving a series of related tasks graded in difficulty and of varying complexity have the advantage of challenging and potentially engaging all students.

Differentiation in group work

There has been a significant increase in the amount of assessed group work on higher education programmes. This is justified in terms of developing the group working skills of students, but is also an understandable pragmatic response to the pressures of having to assess an increased number of students in reduced time and with reduced resources. However, it is often difficult to differentiate an individual's contribution to a group assignment and high achievers in particular may be disadvantaged when assessment methods include some form of group working. Much has been written on how to fairly assess group work using peer and individual assessment, walkthroughs and group viva, and student reflective logs, and how to monitor individual contributions using frequent progress checks and red card/yellow card systems. Useful though these interventions are, group assessment remains problematic. A fairer approach is to set group work so that students may share the research and analysis/organisation of information, but to assess each student individually on a derived individual product.

Conclusion

It is useful when considering how to differentiate the student learning experience to think in terms of learning opportunities rather than learning outcomes. It is vitally important that we always give students the option to go beyond minimal requirements.

It is also useful to consider differentiation at the design stage and to frontload the investment of time and effort in designing challenging, engaging assessments, learning resources and research opportunities that will allow high achieving students to work beyond the curriculum. Redesign your module so that you have an aligned learning programme in which the students have an opportunity to learn to think, and focus on developing student motivation since differentiation requires student self-direction.

Underpinning all that has been discussed in this chapter is a fundamental shift in the role of the lecturer. There is not enough time to effectively differentiate the individual student learning experience alongside all the traditional roles of the tutor. You need to consider becoming a facilitator, a planner of activities and an assessor rather than an instructor. You will need to be prepared for less structure and more interaction than have traditionally been the case. Consider the feasibility and advantages of grouping students by ability, by interest, by learning style or in some other way. Think about ways in which you can differentiate what students are doing in terms of content, process and/or product. This multiple differentiation can make life more interesting both for your students and for you.

Finally, balance the potential advantages of differentiation with the realities of restricted time and resources available to you. Don't make wholesale changes to your programme or module introducing flexible delivery, assessment and curriculum without first considering the knock-on effects of any changes. However, differentiation should engage students more deeply in their learning, providing for constant development and for an exciting and stimulating learning environment. It is certainly worth assessing whether your module can be enhanced to better accommodate the whole range of student learning needs.

10

Addressing student satisfaction

This chapter addresses the following questions:

- What can I do in my teaching to increase my students' satisfaction with their learning?
- How can I ensure that students' increased satisfaction will show from their evaluation responses?

Introduction

Making teaching work is about ensuring that students are satisfied with their learning experience, and that this satisfaction in turn plays its part in enhancing the quality of their learning. All educational institutions have ways of gathering feedback from students, and the data are then analysed and monitored in some detail as a measure of the quality of the teaching. Many of the student evaluation instruments cover very similar dimensions, and in this chapter, we're taking the statements in the UK's National Student Survey (for more information, please see http://www.thestudentsurvey.com/) as an example of the sort of feedback areas which are commonly addressed. Many other countries elicit student experience using a variety of similar instruments, and there is wide discussion about how best to elicit students' views on their experience of higher education. That said, the particular agendas addressed by the National Student Survey make a useful backdrop for our overall suggestions for making teaching work – and for helping students to *feel* that teaching has indeed worked for them.

We don't however suggest that to make teaching work you need to implement *all* of our suggestions in this chapter. Moreover, you are likely to be able to add in your own experience of teaching in your particular discipline to fine tune these suggestions to your own students, and indeed to add suggestions of your own which are even better than ours. This chapter is meant to be a starting point, not an end in itself.

The National Student Survey was used widely in England in 2005 and also included Scottish institutions in 2006, asking students to give their opinions on each of 23 statements, as follows:

For each statement, show the extent of your agreement or disagreement:
5 Definitely agree
4 Mostly agree
3 Neither agree nor disagree
2 Mostly disagree
1 Definitely disagree
N/A Not applicable

The elements of the survey consisted of four statements about 'the teaching on my course', five about 'assessment and feedback', three statements each about 'academic support', 'organisation and management', 'learning resources' and 'personal development', and with two final questions about the overall experience.

The teaching on my course

1 Staff are good at explaining things

Explaining things to students is a central part of making teaching work. But what does 'good at explaining things' boil down to in practice?

We suggest that you:

- Accept that explaining things to students is a key part of your job. Tempting as it might be to reply 'go and look it up' or (more helpfully) 'there's a really good explanation of this on page 35', it is better for you to be seen to be willing to respond immediately to any requests for explanations.
- Be patient, and also willing to explain things at just about any time. While it is useful to be able to explain things to individual students, it is often better if your explaining is done with groups of students (not least as you can then help them to deepen their understanding by explaining it to each other, or by applying the new knowledge together to solve problems). Explaining to individuals can take up too much time, and can advantage those students who are bold enough to ask for explanations over other students who may have just as much need for explanations but who lack the confidence to ask you – or who don't want you to know that they don't yet understand something.
- Keep track of what needs explaining. For example, when individual students ask for particular things to be explained and, after trying to explain to their satisfaction make a note of the topic, and build in short explanation sessions into lectures for the benefit of others who may need the same explanation. This helps the students who sought individual explanations to feel better

about the fact that these were needed, and also gives them a further chance to develop their understanding of the matter being explained.

- Explain in more than one way. For example, by using face-to-face sessions to bring the many extra dimensions into play, including helping students to find out what you mean through your tone of voice, body language, facial expression, gesture, speed of speech, emphasis, and so on.
- Explain it another way when the first way did not completely succeed. This is better than simply repeating your previous explanation.
- Respond to puzzled looks. As you explain things, watch out for the moment when students' eyes show that you've lost them, and then find out from them "What exactly is the bit that's a problem to you here?" Then respond to their replies.
- Explain using more than one medium. For example, as well as explaining things face-to-face to whole groups, write down frequently-needed explanations, and make them available as handouts or web pages.
- Explain using more than one dimension. For example, give explanations a visual dimension when possible, using pictures, cartoons, flowcharts, diagrams, mind-maps, and so on. This can help students who don't catch on to aural explanations on their own.
- Repeatedly enquire whether your explanations have been successful. You need to be careful about the possibility of students simply saying "Yes" to stop us continuing to explain to them. One of the best ways of checking that students have understood your explanations is to get them to explain it back to you – or better still, to each other. The act of explaining something where the light has just dawned is an excellent way to help students to consolidate their grasp of a new concept or idea.

To ensure that students are satisfied with your purposeful efforts to explain things to them, it is useful to remind them of how importantly you regard this aspect of your work, and continually ask them in whole group contexts (for example) "Have my explanations of this worked for you – raise two hands if 'completely', one hand if 'mostly' and no hands if 'not yet'."

2 *Staff have made the subject interesting*

This begs the question 'What does *interesting* actually mean?' Yet, if you ask lots of people, just about everything is deemed 'interesting' by at least some of them. If, however, you've got in your syllabus an area that you know is likely to be found dry – or even boring – by a significant proportion of your students, it's worth taking purposeful steps to add some interest factors wherever possible – or at least to break up the more dreary parts with interesting diversions.

Our suggestions for helping students to feel that you're making the subject interesting for them include:

- Legitimising some parts of the subject being less appealing than others. It's a bad idea to pretend that the difficult bit (or the boring bit, or the routine bit) is really fascinating. Cover it and then go on to explain why the bit concerned is useful or necessary, or how it leads on to other things which are much more exciting.
- Not blaming students for being disinterested. Your own particular subject may actually not be the most remarkable thing that your students are encountering in their studies. Only a few (if any) are likely to end up specialising in your chosen subject.
- Explaining to students why they are doing the 'less interesting' bit. Say what this is for, where it fits into the big picture of the course or module, and where it leads to.
- Addressing the students' question "What's in it for me to master this non-interesting bit?" Explain how it leads to marks in exams or coursework assignments, and how it will help students to be ready to go on to other important things.
- Not being uninteresting for too long at a time. Spice up the less appealing bits of the syllabus with diversions which regain students' enthusiasm. Even taking a minute out using the odd funny slide, or humorous anecdote, can make the difference.
- Finding something which *is* interesting about the less interesting topic. It's worth students remembering this bit even if it's not particularly important, rather than remembering nothing.

3 *Staff are enthusiastic about what they are teaching*

If you don't come across as being enthusiastic about what you're teaching, it's no surprise that students notice this! More importantly perhaps, if other staff come across as passionate about their subjects and you're less up-front with displaying your enthusiasm about our bit of the syllabus, students will notice this, and it will be reflected in their feedback.

Perhaps the worst scenario is where you are *not* enthusiastic about what you are teaching, for reasons such as:

- Enthusiasm being present for your research, and teaching being seen as a bit of a chore, and this coming across to students.
- Teaching a subject not close to your own field of interest, and your indifference to that subject being transmitted to students.
- Having a bad day (week, year) when you're not particularly enthusiastic about anything, and this lack of enthusiasm being evident to students in the context of a particular subject they're trying to learn from you.

- Being new to teaching the topic concerned, and your enthusiasm about the topic being somewhat submerged in your attempts to work out how best to teach it.

So how best can you cause students to believe that you're enthusiastic about what you're teaching? We hope the following suggestions will help.

- When you *are* already enthusiastic about what you're teaching, let it show. Communicate your enthusiasm using tone of voice, body language and (particularly) eye-contact with students. Sentiments such as "The thing that really fascinates me about this is ... " can help students to realise that the subject can indeed be found really interesting, and that the person teaching it is already enthused about it.
- Resist the temptation to let it show when you're *not* enthused about a particular subject area. It's fine to explain to students that something is actually quite difficult, but not so good if students pick up the message that it's not important. If something *isn't* important for your students to learn, it is probably better to miss it out altogether, or at least not spend too much of your valuable face-to-face time on it.

4 The course is intellectually stimulating

How best can you make students feel that what they are learning is 'intellectually stimulating'? What exactly does 'intellectually stimulating' mean in practice? Can *everything* be made intellectually stimulating? What about the problem whereby something which high fliers find intellectually stimulating may be regarded by low fliers as difficult and challenging? As discussed in Chapter 9, it is important to differentiate the student experience to accommodate a variety of learning needs. What about those students where that which is 'challenging' is alternatively looked upon as something problematic rather than something exciting? This overlaps with the 'enthusiasm' agenda addressed above, but is perhaps rather more subtle. The following suggestions may help your students to gain the feeling that your part of their learning is intellectually stimulating.

- Think through the various learning outcomes making up the course elements you teach, and give them a star rating for 'intellectual stimulus' – for example, three stars for the most satisfying outcomes, down to one star for 'not really stimulating'. Then devise your own strategy to help students to see that the less stimulating outcomes serve as a means to the end of the most stimulating outcomes being intellectually satisfying.
- Help your students take pride in their achievements, particularly when they have mastered something which could be regarded as intellectually stimulat-

ing. Help them to feel proud that they have got their heads round difficult concepts and ideas.

- Translate the intended learning outcomes around which your syllabus is based into more stimulating language. Use the phrase "What this really means is … " to justify your translation into more exciting language when appropriate.
- Get your students to think about which parts they have found most 'intellectually stimulating'. For example, ask them to write on Post-its the particular elements they have found most stimulating in your part of their studies so far, and share with them the results of your survey. This may help them to gain a sense of any elements which their peers find intellectually stimulating, and at the same time this will increase the satisfaction of the group as a whole with this dimension of their learning experience.

Assessment and feedback

As discussed in Chapter 8, the results of the National Student Survey in the UK in 2005 and 2006 showed that assessment and feedback were the least satisfactory elements in terms of student satisfaction. Chapter 8 contains suggestions about how to help this situation by improving assessment design, and by paying attention to how well feedback is actually working for students. The following additional suggestions against each of the five statements may help you to further increase student satisfaction with assessment and feedback.

5 The criteria used in marking have been clear in advance

Teaching staff often reply "But they *were* clear in advance!" To ensure that students are more satisfied about this, the following suggestions should help.

- Don't just publish the assessment criteria in student handbooks or on relevant websites. Bring the benefits of tone of voice, body language and eye contact to bear upon the clarity of the marking criteria. Explain them in lectures and tutorials, face-to-face with students. Ask students to ask you questions about how the marking criteria work in practice.
- Give students the chance to apply marking criteria. For example, get them to mark some past work in a whole group setting such as a lecture, using the criteria, before setting out to do some similar coursework, or before they get into revising for related exam questions. In practice, students only *really* know what marking criteria mean when they have tried to make judgements themselves using the criteria.
- Get students to self-assess their own coursework at the point at which they submit it for marking, using the same criteria as will be used for tutor assess-

ment of the work. Then give them feedback about how well their self-assessment has worked in practice, and guidance about particular criteria where there was a gap between the self-assessment and tutor assessment.

6 Assessment arrangements and marking have been fair

Teaching staff often reply to criticism about this with "But the arrangements *were* fair – we strove to ensure this!" Nevertheless, student opinion overall is that there is room for improvement here. The following tactics may help your students to have increased confidence in the fairness of your assessment arrangements and marking.

- Explain to your students the efforts which go into making assessment arrangements and marking as fair as possible. Explain that draft exam questions (for example) are discussed by committees or assessment boards and refined and clarified before being set for students. Explain the role of external examiners or moderators in getting the questions right beyond doubt before students see the questions. A lot of work goes on behind the scenes in making assessment fair, but students often have no idea about how much is done to the questions and marking schemes before they become acquainted with the questions.
- Put yourself into your students' position. Imagine you have got a poor mark of grade, and have felt 'this isn't fair'. Students who feel disappointed with their assessment results may think 'it isn't fair', and this thinking may continue to colour their feelings about assessment and marking overall. The way round this is to make sure that students know exactly *why* they were awarded low marks or grades, and (more importantly) that they get advice about how to improve on these grades in their next piece of work. Feed-forward is particularly important here, not just feedback.

7 Feedback on my work has been prompt

Getting feedback to students promptly has become more of a problem as class sizes have increased. Also, with modular programmes, it is often the case that even two or three weeks' delay in getting feedback to students is too much, as they will have moved on to other aspects of their studies before the feedback reaches them, and will therefore take little or no notice of it. The following suggestions may help you not only to get feedback to your students more rapidly, but also to increase your students' satisfaction with the speed of your feedback.

- Try giving quite a lot of feedback to your students at the point when they submitt their work for assessment, and even before you have started to mark it. A way of doing this is suggested in some detail in Chapter 8.
- Make sure students know they are getting feedback. We may know that we are

giving them feedback, but it is useful to actually say so to them at the time. Use the word 'feedback' often in your discussions with students.

- Where possible, reduce the size of the pieces of work you will mark, for example by setting tight word limits on assignments. Rather than saddle yourself with a pile of 3000 word essays or reports to mark, consider having 300 word critical arguments or 'interpretations'. This also helps to ensure that assessment links to higher-level thinking skills, rather than routine writing skills.

8 I have received detailed comments on my work

Overall, students are not of the opinion that they have received detailed comments on their work. But often in practice, they have indeed received detailed comments and not actually made good use of them. The following suggestions may both help your students to feel that they have received detailed comments *and* ensure that your students make use of these comments.

- Where possible, separate the mark or grade from the feedback comments. For example, give back students' work with feedback comments but no mark, and ask students to work out their mark using the feedback comments to help them. This at least ensures that students do read the feedback comments. Where students then correctly work out their mark or grade (within a reasonable tolerance limit) congratulate them, and (more importantly) find time to discuss marks or grades with students who underestimate or overestimate the value of their work, so that they know what went wrong with their self-assessment of it.
- Use technology to get more feedback comments to large groups of students. For example, use the technique mentioned in Chapter 8 to give students a considerable quantity of *generic* feedback at the point at which they submit their work for marking. Then use some of the time you save (by not having to write similar comments about common mistakes repeatedly on different students' work) to give each student *specific*, useful feedback about their own particular work.
- Use face-to-face contexts such as whole class lectures to give students feedback, bringing the additional dimensions of tone of voice, body language and so on to bear on increasing students' feeling that they have indeed got detailed comments on at least some aspects of their work. Remember to remind them that "This is feedback."

9 Feedback on my work has helped me clarify things I did not understand

The previous two statements are about whether students feel they are getting enough feedback, quickly enough. This statement is about whether the feedback is really working for them. Our suggestions for the previous two statements should also help to make sure that students are benefiting from our feedback, and the following suggestions further add to these.

- Keep asking students about how your feedback is helping them. For example, if you are using a self-assessment pro-forma to get your students to reflect on their coursework at the point at which they submit it, you could include a question or two along the lines of 'Which part of my feedback on your last assignment helped you most to understand something which you had not quite mastered at that point?', and 'What feedback would you particularly find useful on your present assignment?', or 'Which part of this assignment was least clear to you?'
- Use whole group sessions to find out exactly what your students don't yet understand. For example, ask them to write on Post-its their responses to the starter 'The most important thing I don't yet understand is ... ' Then analyse what the most frequently occurring responses are, and go over these aspects with the whole class. Then when marking their related work, make sure that you include feedback comments which relate to any remaining problems with these aspects of the syllabus.

Academic support

The statements in this section relate to student support in general, rather than specific feedback as discussed in the previous section. In some institutions, this means that the support may come from other people as well as subject teachers, in particular study skills support which may be available from a student services section. However, it is likely that students responding to this kind of questionnaire will have uppermost in their minds the support they receive from their teachers, so it is worth setting out to address the agendas underpinning these statements as part of your own efforts to make your teaching work well for your students.

10 I have received sufficient advice and support with my studies

What is 'sufficient'? Many students find it difficult to adjust to study in post-compulsory education, and students from other cultures may have particular problems in adapting to any expectations of independent learning that the institution may have. Probably the best way to help your students feel positive about the quantity of advice and support they receive is to build it directly into your teaching as a matter of course. For example:

- In each teaching session, don't just concentrate on *what* your students are intended to learn, but offer advice regarding *how best* you advise them to go about their learning. For example, don't just suggest "Read Chapter 4 of the textbook." Instead suggest "Use Chapter 4 of the textbook to find out answers to the 25 short questions on the blue handout sheet."

- Keep enquiring in whole group sessions to find out which parts of your syllabus are causing your students most difficulty. For example, give your students a Post-it exercise, asking them to complete the starter 'The piece of advice I most need at the moment is ... '. Don't worry that you will get some spurious responses; the real advice agenda for at least some students will become clearer. When possible, address these difficulties in whole class sessions.
- Encourage students to support each other either informally or through a more formal system of student mentors.

11 I have been able to contact staff when I needed to

Now that it is the case that in many parts of the world students are paying towards the cost of their post-compulsory education, it is not surprising that they can feel short-changed if they find staff difficult to contact when they have questions or worries. However, many of their teachers may in fact be part-time, and others may be heavily involved in research activities during their non-teaching time. The following suggestions may help you to give your students the feeling that you are as readily available as possible to help them.

- Advertise 'office hours' when they are guaranteed to find you. If demand is high, post a 'Sign Your Own Appointment' sheet on your door (or online), so they can 'book' an appointment of five or ten minutes with you. It is usually better to offer quite short appointments, not least so that students don't feel intimidated at the prospect of having to talk to you for too long at a time, but also to help those students who may have many questions to ask to prioritise their needs in advance. In practice, you can always arrange a longer second appointment with those students who really need some extra time from you. If working in a busy shared office, it can be worth booking a classroom or meeting room for these appointments – you can always take some work of your own there to do in between these. Announce your scheduled office hours during each whole group session – students then have no excuse for not knowing how, where and when to find you.
- Encourage emails from students. Set some ground rules for help enquiries, for example 'Short, specific questions please', and agree a timescale in which you will respond to emails. Rather than just reply individually to students, it can be worth posting replies to frequently-asked questions on a discussion board in your institution's virtual learning environment, and replying to the questioner with details of where your response is lodged. This makes sure that stu-

dents who ask a lot of questions (for example about standards of forthcoming exam questions) aren't advantaged over those who aren't so forthcoming in their questions.

- Explain to your students that you're not automatically free to talk to them every time they happen to see you in a corridor or refectory, and that you really want to be helpful to them by giving their needs your full attention and can do this all the better when they can give you advanced notice of what exactly they want to discuss with you and, for example, you can have appropriate 'helpsheets' ready for them when you know what their problems are.
- Try to finish lectures early and let it be known that you are available at the end of the lecture to answer student queries. Often this is the time when issues are at the forefront of learners' minds.

12 Good advice was available when I needed to make study choices

For all sorts of reasons, significant numbers of students end up choosing modules which with hindsight they wished they had not chosen. Sometimes they find that what they believed to be a manageable module turns out to take them out of their depth. Increasing student satisfaction with this aspect of advice is probably something you cannot achieve on your own. The following suggestions may help you to work with others to achieve student satisfaction with study choice guidance.

- As far as you can, make the intended learning outcomes of your modules as transparent as possible, so that students know in advance exactly what is covered, and gain a good idea of the depth and levels concerned. Spell out prerequisites clearly, so that students who need to do some further learning before embarking on your particular module are alerted accordingly.
- Recognise that many students are more interested in the type of assessment they will face than in the content of a particular module. Ensure that students know how they will be assessed.
- Consider bringing in a few students who have already succeeded with your module, to advise potential recruits to the module exactly what it takes to succeed. Some institutions organise a 'module fair' where potential students can find out from staff and past students quite a lot of useful 'between the lines' information about particular choices they may make.
- Ask your existing students to write on Post-its 'Things I wished I'd known before starting on this module' and gather together their responses into a short, sharp guide to the module.

Organisation and management

This section of the UK's National Student Survey is particularly vague! It thus becomes only too easy to pass on the blame for any student dissatisfaction. However, the following suggestions aim to help you to address what you yourself can do to ensure that your students are as satisfied as possible with the issues behind each of the statements in the section.

13 The timetable works efficiently as far as my activities are concerned

Students today face more pressures and more demands on their time than ever before. With many students in part-time employment and with caring and other responsibilities, students need to know their timetable in advance in order to be able to plan other aspects of their lives.

- Where possible negotiate students' timetables with them or at the very least publish timetables well in advance and keep changes to timetables to a minimum.
- From time to time, do a whole class exercise, asking your students to jot down any particular timetabling problems they are experiencing in the context of those parts of the syllabus you are teaching. You won't be able to address all of the responses you may get, but at least you will be able to identify whether there are some timetabling matters which are affecting a significant number of your students adversely, and may perhaps be able to make some adjustments to help them.
- When students have particular problems with timetabling, ask them directly and individually "What may I be able to do to help you with this?" They may at least have some ideas which you can follow through – or at least pass into the system which oversees timetabling in your institution for future reference. And even when you can't help directly, your students may understand why the changes they would like could not be achieved in the short term.

14 Any changes in the course or teaching have been communicated effectively

This is a dimension of student satisfaction you can address more directly. For example:

- Establish communication channels right at the outset. Communicate frequently so that students get into the habit of checking bulletin boards, emails, and so on.

- Make sure that any changes in your own parts of their studies are communicated by all possible means, including announcements in whole group lectures, accompanied by something visual like a slide or overhead for those who respond better to visual stimuli, and a slip of paper given out as a handout for those who will need reminding of what they have heard or seen.
- Also include details of any changes on the Virtual Learning Environment in a 'changes' or 'announcements' section, so that students who aren't present at the relevant whole-group sessions are informed. Make it a ground rule that all students have the responsibility to look at this section of the VLE at least weekly, for example.
- For anything particularly important, it can be worth sending all your students a short email, with a well-chosen message title to ensure that they are going to get the gist of the message before they delete it.
- Where changes to a class are unavoidably made at the last minute take on the responsibility of ensuring all students are contacted. There is nothing much worse than students waiting for a lecturer who doesn't turn up for their class (and these are just the sort of incidents that will spring to mind when asked about effective communication).

15 The course is well organised and is running smoothly

The opportunity for the buck to be passed seems endless here! However, there are indeed some things you can do to ensure that your students feel that their overall course is well organised and runs smoothly. For example:

- Make *your* bits of the course well organised and smoothly run. This is at least partly about giving the impression that *you* are well organised yourself – for example, by being punctual at lectures, tutorials and other teaching-learning sessions, and by always knowing where you left off at a previous session, and so on.
- Don't grumble to students about others not being as well organised as you are, and refrain from empathising with students who may complain that others aren't as helpful as you are (even if secretly you sympathise a lot with your students' grumbles).
- Make your good organisation *visible*. For example, use handouts and bulletin boards to document your efforts to keep the course running smoothly. Front-load your efforts into designing informative module guides, schemes of work and calendars, and save time dealing with ad hoc queries about assignment deadlines and the like.
- Try to ensure that there is consistency of message from staff and that problems and disagreements are dealt with behind the scenes.

Learning resources

At first sight, it can be tempting to say "Not my responsibility" when students express dissatisfaction with the three statements in this section of the survey. However, as an individual teacher, there are indeed things which you can do to lead towards greater student satisfaction with these aspects of their learning experience.

16 The library resources and services are good enough for my needs

- Make sure that you know well in advance exactly what library resources and services your students will need in connection with your parts of the syllabus, and give your library or learning resource centre staff really good notice of your students' requirements. Ask them to assure you that the provision will be in place, and to advise you straightaway if there will be any shortfall, so that you can plan round the situation.
- Where there is a risk that large numbers of students will attempt to borrow particular resources, leading to none being available for others, arrange with your library staff for there to be a 'desk collection' of resources which cannot be borrowed for a particular period.
- Give your students clear advance briefings about the books, articles and resources you expect them to use so that they don't waste their time looking for them, and remind your library or resource centre staff of the expected timing of the demand for these resources.
- Help your students to use the resources really efficiently, by giving really clear briefings about exactly what they should try to do when they use them, rather than have them drifting aimlessly and at a slow pace through the resource materials.

17 I have been able to access general IT resources when I needed to

This may of course be a matter of institutional policy, and some institutions are much better equipped than others. In particular, smaller colleges may not have the range of IT facilities as in larger institutions. So what can you do, as an individual teacher, to address student satisfaction in this area?

- Maximise the efficiency with which your students use the IT resources. You can do this partly by demonstrating in large-group sessions how you expect them to go about particular tasks, and by providing clearly written, step-by-step instructions so that limited resources go that much further.
- If particular resources are limited, check out whether you will be able to secure some related availability in other places, for example local public libraries or

in collaboration with local, larger, higher education institutions. If necessary, make arrangements which simplify the processes of your own students being admitted to the use of these alternative IT resources.

- Consider the possibility of staggering the demand. For example, give a large class three IT resource-based tasks using different resources, with a suggested timetable indicating in which order different students should undertake the respective tasks.

18 I have been able to access specialised equipment, facilities, or rooms when I needed to

The suggestions for the previous two statements continue to apply to student satisfaction with specialised equipment and facilities. However, you can do your own part to minimise problems by considering one or more of the following:

- Make sure that any specialised equipment is really needed by your students, and that it is not just 'icing on the cake' for them. In other words, the use of specialised equipment or facilities should relate very strongly to your students' achievement of one or more particular intended learning outcomes.
- Devise relevant alternative tasks for your students to do at times when they are waiting for their turn to use the specialised equipment or facilities, so that they do not feel that their time is being wasted.
- With larger groups of students, you could consider turning the use of the specialised equipment and facilities into small-group activities, so that the availability of resources will stretch further with your students. This would mean ensuring with those in charge of the resources that group activity would be practicable, and would not disturb other users of the same facilities.

Personal development

The statements collected together under this broad heading tend to relate to students' feelings about their overall personal development as a result of their broad experience during the various elements making up their course, and necessarily some of these personal qualities will be developed further in some course elements more than in others, depending on the particular nature of the curriculum of individual course components.

Therefore, in the suggestions which follow each of the statements in this final part of the UK's National Student Survey, we will concentrate on what *you* can do to ensure that your own contributions to your students' learning experience play their part in developing their overall personal attributes appropriately.

19 The course has helped me to present myself with confidence
20 My communication skills have improved

These two statements overlap so much in practice, that we have provided below some overall suggestions which impact on both confidence and communication skills.

- Where possible, include solo or group presentations and showcasing as part of the overall assessment of the course. When presentations are assessed, students often put a great deal into preparing and giving them, and though they may find this somewhat stressful at the time, they are usually quick to recognise that their confidence has increased as a result of the process. Showcasing allows students to present and discuss their work with a range of individuals.
- Build in informal rehearsals for presentations, before students undertake assessed ones. These can be as short as five minutes, but can still cause students to move forward on their communication skills development.
- Make small-group teaching really participative for students, so that sessions are dominated by their own contributions, in contexts where they don't feel threatened or embarrassed.
- Give students feedback not just on their mastery of the subject, but on the levels of oral and written communication skills which they use in the various contexts where they demonstrate their subject knowledge. In particular focus on feed-forward, helping students to take specific and manageable steps to improve their communication skills from one task to another.
- Ask students throughout the course to reflect upon their communication skills and to track their development.

21 As a result of the course, I feel confident in tackling unfamiliar problems

Problem-solving skills are highly valued in employment, and increasing students' confidence in tackling unfamiliar problems prepares them well for future lifelong learning and continued professional development. Ways of helping students to feel that they are developing such competence include:

- Building short, group problem-solving exercises into students' everyday experience. Students can learn a lot from each other about how to go about solving problems, and their confidence increases particularly when the problem solving is a learning experience for them rather than in an assessment-related context.
- Interspersing your curriculum delivery, even in whole-class sections, with short, unfamiliar problem-solving tasks for students to do in buzz-groups, fol-

lowed by quick debriefing so that students who were not successful in solving the problems don't have long to wait before finding out what they could have done to solve them.
- Setting occasional and informal (non-mandatory) homework exercises consisting of a few unfamiliar problems for students to have a go at solving, perhaps with a small prize for whoever gets the best solutions to you by a given date. Then debrief the exercise, for example with a prepared handout sheet illustrating solutions to all the problems, while at the same time congratulating those students who found particularly interesting solutions of their own.

General considerations

The National Student Survey as used in the UK ends with two questions, the first asking for an overall satisfaction rating regarding the perceived quality of the course, and the second asking for open-ended feedback about particular positive or negative aspects students may wish to give.

22 Overall, I am satisfied with the quality of the course

The suggestions we have already given should lead to improved overall satisfaction, and should help you keep track of students' satisfaction ratings on an ongoing basis through all stages of your teaching. A further way of monitoring students' satisfaction in a broad way is to issue them all with Post-its in a lecture now and then, and to ask them to write the three words 'stop', 'start' and 'continue' on them, then to give you short messages about what they would prefer to stop doing, start doing, and continue doing. The 'stop' responses may alert you to what they perceive as 'negative aspects', in time for you to do something about them – or at least give you the chance to explain *why* it is important for them to be doing some things they are not particularly enjoying. The 'start' elements may give you ideas about some things they would regard as positive developments. Above all, the 'continue' responses help you to see where they are already satisfied. It is useful, after analysing a round of 'stop, start, continue' feedback from your students, to feed back to them the overall findings so that they feel that their feedback is being taken seriously and will be acted upon.

23 Looking back on the experience, are there any particularly positive or negative aspects you would like to highlight?

It is human nature to recall highlights or lowlights of an experience. If you are aware of a particularly weak or negative aspect of the course, then try to address student concerns as soon as they arise to stop the problem from escalating and characterising that course in the minds of your students. By doing so, you may even find students commenting positively on your proactive and prompt response to problems. Consider building a 'highlight' into your course. For example you could arrange a visit or invite a controversial guest lecturer.

Conclusion

Naturally, it gives us pleasure to know that our students are satisfied with their learning experience and the quality of our teaching. However, it is also useful for us to be able to continuously monitor student satisfaction, not least so that we can do something about some of the areas where they express dissatisfaction. Moreover, there are always other people who are interested in data pertaining to student satisfaction (often those staff whose work embraces quality assurance) and it is in our own interests not only to make our teaching work, but to work towards students *saying* that our teaching is working well for them.

11

Finding your feet as a new or part-time member of staff

This chapter addresses the following questions:

- What may I need to find out before I start?
- How can I keep channels of communication with colleagues open?

This short chapter is included particularly for part-time staff, but we hope that it may also be of use to full-time staff especially when taking up a new post.

Increasing proportions of part-time staff

There are now more part-time and sessional staff than ever before working in further and higher education institutions in many parts of the world. These staff are often thrown in at the deep end, with lectures to prepare and deliver, assessments to plan and administer, and small-group teaching to organise and facilitate. They often have relatively restricted opportunities for training and staff development. Part-timers include staff on the following kinds of appointment:

- *Fractional appointments:* the most common of these include 0.2 (equivalent to a day a week), 0.4 (two days a week) and so on. But quite frequently are 0.25 – a bit more than a day a week – and 0.5 – half a week – which are more likely than not in practice to get rounded up to the next whole number of days, unless there are ways of managing to be in an institution for just half a day. Fractional appointments may well involve more than just 'lecturing', and may include associated duties relating to setting and marking assessed work and exams. One bonus about fractional appointments is that it is quite likely that the normal terms and conditions applying to full-time posts will continue to apply, not least holiday entitlement, sick pay, and so on.

- *Visiting lecturers:* this can mean just about anything, ranging from coming in to give the odd lecture now and then, to spending all of a few weeks or even months in the institution concerned. The entitlements to holidays, sick pay and so on are likely to be written into the individual details for such appointments. Such appointments may or may not include assessment-related activities, especially in institutions where examiners are required to have gone through training relating to these parts of their work.
- *Occasional lecturers:* this sort of post may resemble 'visiting lecturers' above in some respects, but it is likely that the work involved is even more sporadic, and possibly fixed around particular milestones in the delivery of particular programmes.
- *Specialist tutors:* the terms of reference encompassed by this can include more or less full-time appointments, relating to a narrowly-defined range of work. But equally, specialist tutors could find themselves employed on a part-time basis, as and when the need for their particular specialism manifests itself in the delivery of courses or programmes.
- *Guest lecturers:* this implies appointments which are *very* part-time, for example including the terms and conditions for going to an institution on a one-off occasion to deliver a particular lecture (or seminar or tutorial and so on) to a particular audience (students, or staff, or both) for a particular purpose (for example, to present an authoritative account of a topic which the person concerned is distinguished in).
- *Casual staff:* this term is seldom used for lecturers (even when their terms and conditions could be considered to be 'casual' or 'temporary'), and is more often used for additional staff employed to help out with peak demand in other areas of the work of an institution (ranging from student support services, to secretarial and administrative support, and other kinds of job).
- *Sessional staff:* when this term is used regarding lecturers, the main reason seems to be that the appointments only relate to 'sessions' – in other words, terms or semesters when the students are in attendance in the institution concerned. The staff may be employed without any consideration of holiday pay, and may be expected to engage in other activities to support themselves outside of session times.
- *Teaching Assistants (or Graduate Teaching Assistants):* like 'sessional staff' in most respects, with duties relating to teaching and perhaps nothing between terms and semesters. However, such posts are often combined with research activities, which may fill in the times between teaching sessions.
- *Demonstrators:* particularly in subjects involving laboratory or field work demonstrators have teaching duties, and sometimes even assessment-related duties, but are likely to be involved in research for the remainder of their time.
- *Project officers:* such personnel may be employed on fixed-term research con-

tracts, or short-term funded projects relating to teaching, learning and assessment, but their actual teaching work may be secondary to the principal focus of their appointments.

All of the above involve teaching duties on a scale of something less than 'full-time appointments'. However, particularly in research-led institutions, many lecturers consider themselves as only part-time due to the extent of the teaching (and assessment-related activities) they undertake, when their main job is research. Even though they may work in an institution for most of the year, they can feel themselves to be part-time teachers in at least some respects.

One hundred assorted questions which new and part-time staff may need to have answered

We mentioned above that many more part-time staff are employed nowadays in post-compulsory education. Sometimes it is difficult for them to find their feet, especially when joining a large institution. At Leeds Metropolitan University, we prepare a checklist for them, to help them find out the answers to many of the questions they may have, and then sort out which questions they need to follow up in more detail.

Especially if you're starting as a part-timer, you may find this checklist helpful in getting going. (Even if you're a full-time member of staff, there may be questions in the checklist which you should research too).

Question		Answer	Action if needed
1	Where do I go on my first day?		
2	Who do I report to?		
3	What forms do I need to complete to get paid?		
4	When can I expect that to be?		
5	Can I get an advance in the first month?		
6	Is there a loan scheme for public transport?		
7	Where can I park my car legitimately/safely?		
8	What documents do personnel need from me?		
9	If I want to join the union, how do I go about it?		
10	Am I entitled to sick pay if I am ill?		

Question	Answer	Action if needed
11 Do I get any paid holidays?		
12 Are there set hours I am expected to work?		
13 Am I entitled to join the pension scheme?		
14 How do I get my staff ID card?		
15 Do I need a swipe card for door locks?		
16 Which room(s) am I teaching in?		
17 How long do I need to allow to get between rooms?		
18 Where can I get a cup of tea/food?		
19 Where can I make work-relatd phone calls?		
20 Where are the nicest toilets for me to use?		
21 Where can I leave my bike?		
22 Is there anywhere on site I can get a shower?		
23 Is there a secure locker I can use for my possessions?		
24 Where can I keep my coat/outer wear when I'm teaching?		
25 Is there a staff room I can use?		
26 Is there a tea fund I can join or does everyone bring their own tea/coffee?		
27 Do I need to bring in my own mug?		
28 Where do I get keys if I'm locked out of teaching rooms?		
29 What time do the cleaners need to get into the rooms?		
30 Who do I ring if I get locked into the building?		
31 Who do I tell if the room gets really cold in the evening?		
32 How do I get duplicating done?		
33 Where can I get stationery supplies?		
34 Where is the nearest photocopier?		
35 Do I need a code for the photocopier?		
36 Are there limits on how many copies I can make?		
37 What are the copyright constraints on me copying things for students?		
38 Who do I tell if the copier jams?		

Question	Answer	Action if needed
39 Is there an institutional policy on recycling?		
40 Where do I recycle paper/cans/glass/toner cartridges?		
41 Do I have access to a computer on site?		
42 How do I go about getting a computer ID?		
43 Which printer serves the PC on my desk?		
44 Where do I get spare PC consumables (toner cartridges, paper etc)?		
45 What are the rules about using email for my own use?		
46 Can I get any administrative support?		
47 Are there any meetings I need to come to?		
48 Do I get paid for attending?		
49 Can I come to staff development events?		
50 Are they in my own time or in paid-for time?		
51 Am I expected to undertake any training or CPD in teaching and learning techniques?		
52 Am I entitled as a staff member to join language classes/use the sports facilities/get any discounts anywhere?		
53 Where is the library?		
54 How do I get a library card?		
55 How may books am I entitled to borrow?		
56 Can I get inter-library loans?		
57 Who is the Vice Chancellor, Dean, Head of Department?		
58 Who is the staff representative on the academic board?		
59 Who is the union rep?		
60 Who is my course leader?		
61 How do I know if I have any disabled students in my class for whom I need to make reasonable adjustments?		
62 Who do I go to if I am worried about a student?		
63 To whom can I refer on students who tell me about their real concerns?		
64 Who can I consult if I have a very disruptive student?		

Question	Answer	Action if needed
65 Am I allowed to send students out of the class?		
66 How do I find a first-aider if I need one?		
67 Who can help me after hours/in vacations if I have a security worry?		
68 Are there any rules about going out for a drink with the students after work?		
69 Am I expected to keep a register?		
70 Is it my responsibility to inform the course leader if students miss classes?		
71 What are my responsibilities in relation to marking student work?		
72 What are the dates of the assignments?		
73 Will I get any training in assessment?		
74 Will someone check up on/moderate my grading?		
75 What do I do if I suspect a student is cheating/plagiarising?		
76 Am I allowed to give students extensions on written work?		
77 Where do students hand in work for marking?		
78 Where do I collect work that needs marking (and hand it back when it's marked)?		
79 Is it my responsibility to enter marks onto the database?		
80 Am I expected to go along to exam boards?		
81 Do I have to meet the external examiner?		
82 What do I have to do about, assessing students who have notified us about disabilities?		
83 Am I expected to collect student feedback about my teaching?		
84 Is there an institutional course questionnaire?		
85 Who do I pass student feedback on to?		
86 Will anyone come and watch me teaching?		
87 If so, what will their role be?		
88 Who do I tell if I need to report in ill?		
89 What will happen to my classes if I do?		
90 What do I do if I know I am going to miss a class e.g. for a hospital appointment?		

Question	Answer	Action if needed
91 Is it my responsibility to organise a replacement?		
92 What are the dates of the institutional holidays?		
93 Is the building locked up in this period, or can I get to my room?		
94 Do I get allocated a mentor?		
95 How do I find out who my colleagues are?		
96 Do you run any departmental or faculty social events?		
97 When and where is the Christmas party?		
98 Do we work any of the bank holidays?		
99 What happens at the end of my contract?		
100 Who do I tell if I want to leave before my contract is complete?		

Ten ways part-timers can go about communicating with colleagues

One of the problems of being a part-timer is that it's easy to miss out on what's going on around you. This is not least because when you *are* in, you're likely to be busy doing something. The following suggestions may help you to keep up with what you need to know.

1 *Choose a friend*. It's easier to keep up to date with one colleague, than to try to catch up with everyone. Choose someone with considerations such as the following in mind:
   - Someone you're likely to be able to see most times you're in – in other words, usually not a fellow part-timer.
   - Someone who seems good at knowing what is going on.
   - Perhaps your line manager – or perhaps someone else – depending on what sort of person your line manager turns out to be.
   - Someone who will make it his or her business to keep copies of anything important, and put them in your mailbox or on your desk.
   - Someone who will copy you in to email correspondence about meetings and so on, with short notes about what *you* should bear in mind from what's going on.
   - Someone who will not mind you emailing or ringing up to check whether there is anything you should be aware of, when you're not going to be around for a while.

2 *Learn from the experience of other part-timers*. You may need to go a little out of your way to do this, as it may be the case that they are not in when you are – or you may be hot-desking with one or more of them. However, if they've already been there some time before you started, there will be lessons they've learned which can save you time and energy, so it's worth making contact, and preferably meeting up from time to time perhaps in a coffee bar (or pub) rather than at your work base – not least so you can chat about everyone else who affects your work.
3 *Share the job of keeping in touch with other part-timers*. If there are enough of you, you can form a useful network, and save each other time by sharing the load of keeping up with what's going on.
4 *Make it easy for everyone to know how to leave paperwork for you*. For example, ask everyone either to leave bits of paper in your pigeonhole – or in a tray on your desk – but not all sorts of different places.
5 *Get yourself copied into email lists*. Even when most of the emails and notices may not be relevant to you directly, get into the habit of deleting or archiving those which are not relevant, and create folders for the things you feel you will need to have at your fingertips in due course.
6 *Pick up emails remotely if you can*. Most institutions have remote access to emails, and being able to access your correspondence can often make all the difference between being able to stay at home for a day, rather than going in for something which did not actually need your physical presence.
7 *Create a way of letting colleagues know exactly when you will next be 'in'*. The out-of-office reply facilities on email software are good for this purpose – but make sure you do indeed appear when people have been led to believe that you will. Also, sticking a Post-it to your computer monitor with 'Next here: Friday 12th October' can be useful for anyone who calls by on the off-chance of seeing you at your desk. But don't stick it on the screen – it's usual for part-timers' computers to get hot-desked while you're not there.
8 *Try to go to the right meetings*. There are likely to be lots of meetings which aren't really relevant to you as a part-timer, but now and then there may be one where your work is directly relevant. When that happens, it can be worth being there if you can, even if it's not one of your scheduled days – you may indeed be able to take a day off in lieu at some other time.
9 *Try to catch up on all the other meetings*. Keep track of when these are, and make it your business to check with one or two colleagues and find out if anything was agreed which has a bearing on your own work.
10 *Find ways of making it clear when you're out of contact*. As a part-timer, there may be times when you're working for some other institution or organisation, or out of the country on holiday. Using email out-of-office replies, it can be useful on such occasions to say 'Thanks, but I won't actually get your mes-

sage until Monday 7th May' and so on, so that people who attempt to leave you urgent messages are under no delusions about whether you may happen to pick them up in the interim.

Conclusion

You may need to remind yourself, if you're a part-timer, that as far as your students are concerned, you're just one of many teachers they will meet. It's not their business to accommodate any difficulties you encounter as a part-time member of staff, and you can do every bit as much to enhance their learning experience by making your teaching work along the lines we've advocated throughout this book.

12

Putting your best foot forward

This chapter addresses the following questions:

- How can I best show that I have planned systematically and effectively to make my teaching work well?
- When someone is inspecting or observing my teaching, how can I make sure that I do justice to my preparations?

Introduction

Post-compulsory education is frequently subject to external scrutiny by a variety of agencies including, for example, in the UK the Higher Education Funding Council for England, and the Quality Assurance Agency (QAA) (http://www.qaa.ac.uk/), in New Zealand the New Zealand Qualifications Authority (http://www.nzqa.govt.nz/), and in Australia the Australian Universities Quality Agency (http://www.auqa.edu.au/). In addition, professional and subject bodies, like nursing councils, law societies and engineering and accountancy bodies have their own review requirements. It is imperative to put forward a strong and convincing case, built on sound evidence, to demonstrate that programmes of study are appropriate, challenging, fit-for-purpose and clearly articulated for students, staff, employers and other stakeholders. Furthermore, most national higher and further education bodies expect organisations to have their own arrangements for quality assurance and enhancement which anticipate external review and provide security and confidence in educational provision on offer.

You need to be well-prepared for these reviews, as a necessary part of not just making your teaching work, but also in helping your teaching to be *seen* to be working well. The first section of this chapter covers preparation of materials and lessons at the outset and the second section explores preparing for the review itself.

Section 1: personal curriculum design

Preparing learning outcomes

Intended learning outcomes are at the heart of the ways that the curriculum is expressed in outcomes-based education systems that have grown up on several continents. The trend towards outcomes-based education can be tracked back to the Behaviourist school of thought in psychology, and to the quest for precision in training programmes in military contexts in the USA and UK from the 1970s onwards. Basing ideas about learning on what learners are able to *do* to demonstrate what they have learned was even written about by the Greeks and Chinese well over two thousand years ago. There is nothing new about the idea of experiential learning, and outcomes-based education!

In past times, most higher education syllabi were descriptive paragraphs listing the content of what was expected to be 'covered' by a series of lectures (and any associated small-group, practical, or fieldwork, plus independent study by students *reading* for a degree). There was little indication of depth of study, or of how long students should expect to study to become prepared for the assessment which would measure their attainment. There was little if any indication of what students may reasonably expect that they should be come able to do, to show that they had mastered the syllabus to an appropriate level – first class, second class, third class, or fail. Students were somehow expected to *know* what they should do. Those who did know what they should do (or had guessed successfully what they should do) usually passed. Some of those who couldn't work out where the goalposts lay, failed, not because they couldn't master the syllabus, but because they couldn't work out where these goalposts were.

As students gradually evolved into consumers, the expectation grew that their lecturers should 'cover' the syllabus, and that all that should be necessary to gain a degree was to be able to give enough of what the lecturers covered back to them in exam answers and coursework assignments. The corollary was, naturally, that if lecturers didn't cover it, the students wouldn't be expected to give it back, and therefore there was no need to spend time learning it.

However, this trend was overtaken by the information explosion and the communications revolution. Thirty years ago, most students attending a lecture could leave with no more than a few hundred words' worth of information which they had managed to capture during the hour or so of the lecture – and often a great deal less. They would write these words (and in some subjects, numbers, equations, graphs and diagrams) down from what the lecturer said, what questions students asked, the answers to those questions, and occasionally from what the lecturer wrote on a board or projected onto a screen.

Nowadays, with handouts in lectures, or before lectures, or after lectures, and with slides available on intranets, students can gain many thousands of words' worth of information about a mere hour of their learning experience. But this remains just as information – it does not magically transform itself into students' knowledge until they have processed it – made it their own – argued with it – rearranged it – linked it to other information – and so on. The amount 'covered' by lectures has therefore increased dramatically – or at least the amount of *information* resulting from lectures has increased. Perhaps this is partially responsible for the growing expectation among students that their lecturers will 'cover' the syllabus for them? But at the same time, contact hours between students and lecturers have decreased as student numbers have grown, and as the unit of funding resource per hour of contact has diminished in real terms. So teachers have less time to 'cover' the syllabus.

A vital element of making teaching work is to plan for students to leave each teaching-learning encounter with important elements of learning pay-off, which would have been missed if they had merely tried to make sense of the relevant information on their own from books, websites, articles and handouts. In other words, the learning events which spotlight important parts of the syllabus need to have tangible and important *intended learning outcomes*. These are the intended outcomes of being there and participating in a learning event – not just an information-receiving occasion.

A twelve-point plan for getting the learning outcomes right

1. *Start formulating learning outcomes early in the planning process for your teaching.* Good learning outcomes can't be cobbled together in haste (this has too often led to stale learning outcomes!).
2. *Value the process of designing your learning outcomes.* Don't regard it as a chore. The process of thinking through exactly what your students should be aiming to achieve helps you design *how* they will go about their learning, and throws light on how best *you* can set out to make your teaching work well.
3. *Work with your colleagues to get the intended learning outcomes right.* Outcomes are rarely wonderful when designed by individuals working in isolation.
4. *Don't get so fixated on the 'outcomes' bit that you forget about the 'learning'.* The learning outcomes should support rather than detract from the learning process.
5. *Think about how students can make really good use of learning outcomes to inform and guide their study.* Help them to unlock the secrets of the learning process. Consider using learning outcomes quite overtly in lectures and on handouts, in assignment/task briefings and as part of web-based learning resources.
6. *Consider who* else *can use learning outcomes to good effect.* Placement supervisors, potential employers, potential sponsors, recruitment staff, external

examiners, moderators or curriculum reviewers, professional and subject bodies and funders.

7 *Think hard about the language used.* Avoid triviality, banality, imprecision, excessive complexity, academic language, jargon. If your students know exactly what the learning outcomes actually mean, anyone looking at the quality of your teaching and curriculum design will also get the right messages from your outcomes.
8 *Make the outcomes reasonably specific.* But not so specific so as to give the students no space for creativity. Don't get too fixated on performance standards and conditions.
9 *Keep thinking about how you will best be able to measure the outcomes.* How will you be able to align them with authentic assessment tasks? How can they inform the design of assessment criteria?
10 *Keep doing a reality check.* Can the students achieve the outcomes? Can teachers and examiners feasibly make decisions about whether the outcomes have been achieved? Will external scrutineers be happy with the outcomes?
11 *Think about the time frame.* Can your students reasonably achieve your intended learning outcomes in the time available? Can you, through your teaching, help them to achieve the outcomes in the time you have available?
12 *Don't allow your intended learning outcomes to get stale.* Return regularly to them and refresh/reframe as required: they should be live documents.

Preparing lesson plans

'Lesson planning' may make you think back to secondary education, where inspection systems such as those operating in the UK spotlight the preparation of quite detailed lesson plans, which are used as a basis for assessing how well teachers design, conduct and evaluate individual elements of learning. In post-compulsory education, 'lesson' can be broadened to include lectures, seminars, tutorials, practical work elements, and most of the other elements of learning. Furthermore, the same kinds of planning are needed for other contexts of learning where the teacher may be less evident, including independent study using learning resource materials, online learning, and so on.

Everyone will have their own approach to lesson preparation: some like to plan each element, allocating so many minutes to this component and activity and so many to that. Others prefer to have an overall shape to a session in mind and improvise within it. However, for the purposes of external scrutiny, your lesson plans need to combine these approaches to some extent. A common mistake among relatively new teaching staff is over-specification, leaving little leeway to follow up individual student questions and interests. Good lesson plans should have a clear structure to act as a framework, but should also have built-in flexibility to enable the teacher to adapt the class as circumstances require.

The 'Teaching Plan' proforma below has been adapted from Quinn (2000: 193–4) and provides a starting point for following through from the intended learning outcomes for a particular teaching element, so that you can plan in more detail to make your teaching work, and to ensure that your students learn effectively.

Teaching Plan: Part 1	
Title of session	
Kind of session (lecture, seminar, etc)	
Duration of session	
Date	
Venue requirements	
Details of students	
Types of students	
Programme and level	
Number of students	
Aims and intended learning outcomes	
Overall aim of session	
Intended learning outcomes	

Venue and resources	
Resources and equipment required	
Nature of room required	
Your preferred layout for the venue	

Teaching Plan: Part 2			
Draft sequence of activities and processes			
Timing	Content	What you plan to do	What you plan to get your students to do
Your own particular thoughts and questions relating to the planned session as above:			

Section 2: advance preparation for inspection or observation

Prepare for the expected

It is all too easy to forget about external scrutiny until it is imminent, but this is not normally the best course of action. Usually individuals and course teams will have advance warning of the timing of review processes, and even short-notice visits, where, for example, inspectors give only a few days' warning of an inspection visit, but the processes themselves are well-publicised in advance. Everyone in a post-compulsory teaching role should therefore receive training and induction about what they are likely to experience in terms of internal and external review. Where this is not provided, it is a good idea for individuals to do a bit of research for themselves, seeking out institutional and course documentation which outlines the relevant processes. In universities in the UK, for example, there are normally academic boards, academic committees or similar and the secretaries of these bodies will be able to offer you guidance on what kinds of review processes are relevant for your particular subject. Often the minutes of such bodies are available on the intranet or institutional web-page so you could refer to these for background information.

Keeping your own good records

Generally the most important task for an individual in preparing for a review is to be able to produce the right bits of paper for an evidence-collection activity. You should start from your first day of teaching to keep a well-organised paper or electronic file, which might include, for example:

- Accurate records of student interaction, including class-lists for each group you teach. In some institutions, you are expected to keep attendance lists or registers. Increasingly these are held and recorded electronically, and may be monitored by student-liaison officers or similar, since attendance is known to be linked to completion rates. However, it is likely to be useful for you to keep records yourself of who is in your class, particularly when it comes to recording marks for assessed work. If you are a personal tutor or academic coach for a group of students, it is really very helpful to keep records of individual encounters, including off-the-cuff corridor conversations, particularly if a student requests mitigating circumstances support for late or uncompleted work, and claims that you were made familiar with the context. Many also find it helpful to have photos of individual students alongside written records to help remember who is who. If students don't supply these readily on request, it may be possible to download these from an institutional central records, since most student now have ID cards including photos and these may be held centrally.

- Course or module outlines, indicating the range and scope of material taught for each group you teach. You may also be asked to provide schemes of work, lesson plans or other written confirmation of what happens in your classes. While these can be fabricated post hoc just before the inspector arrives (this process is well-known to inspectors and is known as the 'wet ink syndrome'), it is less stressful all round if you keep them up to date as a matter of routine.
- Information about how you assess your students, including assignment briefs, marking schemes, arrangements for moderation of marks and similar. Very clear and accurate records of all student assignments you have marked, including sample formative feedback, are sometimes required so evaluators can see that students are well-supported by detailed information on individual performance, together with guidance on how students can remediate errors and improve grades. You may also be asked for comparative information about student achievement, including ranked lists of student marks and breakdowns of proportions of students receiving each band of marks (in the English system, for example, how many firsts, upper seconds, lower seconds, thirds and fails are awarded in any cohort).
- Records about your own performance as a teacher including, for example, outputs of teaching observations (see below), appraisals and mentor reviews.
- Student evaluation comments. These could be informal comments (letters, cards, emails from grateful students) together with more formal outputs from a variety of evaluation processes including module, course, programme and institutional evaluations (see Chapter 10 for more details of how to address and increase your students' satisfaction with their learning experience).

Being observed teaching

Some people find it terrifying, or at the least off-putting, to have an observer in the classroom evaluating interaction with students. However, it is worth remembering that teachers working in post-compulsory education are watched in their teaching by adults every day, since students themselves are capable of making value judgments about teaching quality (and frequently do). Having a well-prepared and well-qualified colleague sitting in alongside the students should not therefore be regarded as an additional burden, but rather as a potential benefit.

Good practice in teaching observation involves three phases: preparation, the observation itself and review. If you find out you are likely to be observed teaching at some stage, it's a good idea to prepare as much as you can in advance by:

1 *Getting hold of the documentation that describes the particular process being practised*. Will the observer stay in for the whole lesson, for example, or will s/he just come in for a shorter period of time? Is the purpose of the observation evaluation or monitoring? Will s/he take the role of participant, joining in with activities, or will s/he just observe? Will s/he talk to students about your normal classroom practices or will the evaluation be based exclusively on the session observed? Will the focus be on your performance or the student activities?
2 *Having a practice run with a trusted colleague or mentor*. Do this using exactly the same protocols as will be used by the external reviewer. You might like the rehearsal reviewer to focus on something you are particularly concerned about, for example, audibility, pacing, or effectiveness of use of PowerPoint slides. Try if possible to get rehearsal observations of different kinds of activities including (as relevant) lab supervision, practical classes, seminars, lectures, problem classes and so on, so you will be prepared for any eventuality.
3 *Observing one or more colleagues teaching*. Using the same observation pro-formas as will be used in the actual review occasion. Research on peer-observation shows that the observer often gains more than the observee, so simply watching others teaching is likely to help you see what an external scrutineer might be looking for, and might build up your own confidence levels.
4 *Making a video of yourself in action with a class*. Review this at leisure using the observation protocols so you can evaluate your performance for yourself. It's probably best not to do this until a friend or colleague has observed you though, as most people hate seeing themselves on video and tend to concentrate on superficial negatives rather than the underlying performance.

Setting the scene

On another level, there is further preparation to be done in relation to the session itself. If you can, tell the students what is going on. Sometimes student groups get rattled, particularly if they think it is themselves who are being observed rather than the teacher, so putting them in the picture might help them to be more natural. Don't try to over-coach students in advance, since this is often very obvious to the observer. One common problem is that students, wanting to be helpful, may keep very quiet in an observed class and you may have more problems than normal in getting them to interact with you in question and answer sessions. Remember that ultimately the students' needs must come first and concentrate on helping them learn as normal, rather than putting on a big performance.

Without going over the top, you need to prepare presentations and other materials for an observed class to the best of your ability. It's hard to do this, but try to remain as level-headed as possible and don't aim too much for an all-singing, all-dancing performance. Don't, for example, try to incorporate highly-technological elements into a session if this is not your natural forte. Equipment seems to sense high-stress situations and will let you down in the most embarrassing way if you attempt to go beyond your own technological capability for the sake of putting on a good show. Always have a contingency plan for any technological elements in such circumstances.

It's a good idea to go into the room in which your teaching will be observed well beforehand, to check you are confident in the use of the sound system, lighting, data projection and heating/air conditioning units prior to the session. If you plan to use handouts, decide in advance whether these will be handed out or collected as students enter the room or when they leave. If students need them during the session, you may like to give them out round the room in advance to ensure speedy distribution. For this observed session, throw environmental caution to the wind and prepare plenty of extra copies so you don't run out. Have a couple of spare copies in large print on hand for any students with visual impairments and consider using cream paper with dark blue text, since this is regarded as being helpful for some students with dyslexia. Actually, this is good practice you should observe in all sessions, not just observed ones, but it does no harm to do it especially for this session and point out your good inclusive practice to students (and the observer) at the start of the session.

On the day of the observation

You may well feel better about the process if you are sure you have some control over the situation. If possible, talk to the observer in advance and establish how the process will work and things like where the observer will sit. If this is not possible, label a seat near the back of the room for the observer (they usually like to sit where they can watch students as well as you in action).

Timing of sessions also can go strangely adrift when someone is watching you, so be prepared to have material in readiness to include if you are going at a rapid pace because of nerves, but which can be dropped if you are running out of time. If you provide your presentation slides as a handout, tell the students (and the observer) at the start of the session that you are unlikely to use all of them during the session and that any additional slides are intentional 'bonus features' for subsequent review. It is important that no one (observer or students) should think that some slides were missed out due to mis-timing. Think well in advance about how your session will finish, since it is often first and last impressions that make the most impact.

After the observation

In some observation schemes, the observer will give you immediate feedback and in others, nothing will be said. If you are given feedback, keep a note of what is said to you since it is all too easy in the heat of the moment to hear and then forget what is said. Don't hesitate to ask for clarity about unclear points but don't be tempted to challenge or argue with the observer, as this rarely improves the situation. If some negative feedback is given, try not to dwell on it since any observation is simply a snapshot and cannot fully reflect your total capability. This is the point at which you should refer back to your file of positive comments from students (see above), to help you to recover your equilibrium. Remember also that when reflecting on any teaching session, there are always things that could have been improved with hindsight, and that it is useful to note such things routinely, to help towards continuously making your teaching work even better.

Conclusion

It is always a deep learning experience for us when we have our teaching observed, and receive feedback on how well our teaching is working – or otherwise! Emotions can run high, and it is easy to become over-sensitive to critical comments. We hope, therefore, that some of our suggestions in this chapter will help you to get the most from teaching observation, and allow you to use feedback to make your teaching work even better as you develop your mastery of working with students to help them to learn.

13

Onward and upward!

We hope that you have found in this book answers to some of your questions about teaching smarter, to help you to make your teaching work well. As we have stressed throughout, our main target is to do what we can to make sure that your students' learning happens effectively, efficiently and not least, enjoyably.

If we were to offer succinct advice as to how to make your teaching work we would suggest as a basis the following:

Four steps toward making your teaching work

1 Put yourself in your students' shoes

You are likely to be dealing increasingly with more diverse and more demanding students. Don't assume that your own norms are universal. Invest time in getting to know your students. Listen to them. Learn their names. Find out why they are studying on the programme and what issues they are having to deal with. Many of your students will have no idea what to expect from higher education, so ensure that your students understand the 'rules of the game'. Try to imagine what it must be like to be a student today. Look carefully at the demands you are making upon students and the support available to them. Consider the feasibility and desirability of making learning more flexible. Explain why you are doing things and the point of any work you are asking them to do. Students are more likely to engage if they understand how something fits with their learning needs.

2 Ensure you are in step with your students

Allow students to learn-by-doing and as a priority build in opportunities for regular formative feedback and feed-forward. Ensure students have time in their programme to reflect and make sense of what they have learned, rather than bombarding them with mountains of content and over assessing them. Individuals learn in different ways, so use a variety of channels and resources to transmit your enthusiasm and to assess your students' learning. Once you have developed a relationship with your students it is easier to work in partnership with them, to identify how best to motivate them and to work on their individual learning needs.

3 Step aside

You need to make learners better at learning for themselves and in order to do this you must be willing to step aside and act as a facilitator of learning. Your primary role changes from instructor to provider of learning opportunities and assessor. You may need to move away from traditional models that encourage student dependence upon you and instead invest resources in providing a learning environment that encourages students to explore, experiment and reflect. Look to reduce the time you spend on preparation, delivery and marking and redirect this time to designing engaging assessment tasks and to developing students as independent learners.

4 Take one step at a time

Above all, think about how you can make your life more manageable! All too often initiatives come along that promise much, but turn out to be Trojan horses requiring significant amounts of your time and energy with little return for your efforts. In recent times many lecturers have found themselves overwhelmed by their efforts to incorporate new technologies into their modules whilst at the same time continuing to carry out their traditional roles of lecturer, tutor, seminar leader, marker and material designer in just the same way as always.

Before embracing a trend think carefully about the implications for your workload and consider what trade-off there will be. Don't commit yourself to daily individual emails to your 300 students or to making yourself available online 24/7 without considering what this actually means and precisely what the learning benefits will be for your students. This book suggests many steps you may wish to take to make your teaching more effective. Consider piloting one or two of them and see if they work for you. Always ask yourself what you are going to *stop* doing when you are investing effort elsewhere. If you develop or source online learning objects do you still need to lecture? If you are investing time in getting to know your students and working with them as individuals do you need to focus as much effort on attendance monitoring and plagiarism detection? If you introduce more formative assessment do you still need as much summative assessment and all the associated marking overheads?

And finally...

We hope that the ideas in our book will play at least some part in helping you to gain greater satisfaction – and indeed pleasure – from your teaching. However, this is just a book. It remains important, in your mission to make your teaching really work, to use people as well as ideas on pages such as these. We would encourage you to take every opportunity to discuss your teaching, feedback and assessment with your own colleagues, your students, and anyone else who can help you to think about it all. Keep looking out for other people's experiences you can build on, and particularly for the wisdom some of them have developed through lots of practice, experience, experimenting, and trial and error. Making teaching work is about making wise choices, and choosing tactics you can build into your own teaching strategy. Finally, we hope that you may gain appropriate rewards arising from the recognition that you really make teaching work for your students.

References, further reading and useful websites

Atherton, J.S. (2002) *Heterodoxy: Against Objectives*. Available at: http://www.doceo.co.uk/heterodoxy/objectives.htm (accessed: 24 January 2007).

Biggs, J. (2003) *Teaching for Quality Learning at University* (2nd edition). Maidenhead: Society for Research into Higher Education/Open University Press.

Boud, D. (1990) 'Assessment and the promotion of academic values', *Studies in Higher Education*, 15 (1): 101–11.

Bowl, M. (2003) *Non-traditional Entrants to Higher Education: 'They Talk About People Like Me.'* Stoke on Trent: Trentham.

Braun, D. and Merrien, F.X. (eds) (1999) *New Managerialism and the Governance of Universities in a Comparative Perspective*. London/Philadelphia: Jessica Kingsley.

Brown, S., Rust, C. and Gibbs, G. (1994) *Strategies for Diversifying Assessment in Higher Education*. Oxford: The Oxford Centre for Staff Development.

Carless, D., Joughin, G. and Liu, N-F. (eds) (2006) *How Assessment Supports Learning – Learning-oriented Assessment in Action*. Hong Kong: Hong Kong University Press.

Coffield, F., Moseley, D., Hall, E. and Ecclestone, K. (2004) *Learning Styles and Pedagogy in Post-16 Learning – A Systematic and Critical Review*. London: Learning and Skills Research Centre (downloadable from www.lsn.org.uk). (For a shorter review, see also Coffield, F., Moseley, D., Hall, E. and Ecclestone, K. (2004) *Should We Be Using Learning Styles? What Research Has to Say to Practice*. London: Learning and Skills Research Centre, also downloadable from www.lsn.org.uk)

DfES (2003) *The Future of Higher Education* (UK Government White Paper). Available at http://www.dfes.gov.uk/hegateway/strategy/hestrategy/pdfs/DfES-HigherEducation.pdf (accessed January 2007).

Dribben, N. (2006) *What is Music?* http://www.open2.net/historyandhearts/arts/music251204.html

Fleming, N. and Baume, D. (2006) 'Learning Styles again: VARKing up the right tree!', *Educational Developments*, 7 (4).

Gibbs, G. and Simpson, C. (2002) *Does Your Assessment Support Your Students' Learning?* Milton Keynes: Open University. Available at http://www.brookes.ac.uk/services/ocsd/l_ocsld/lunchtime_gibbs_3.doc (accessed January 2007).

Goleman, D. (1998) *Working with Emotional Intelligence*. London: Bloomsbury.

Guest, E. and Mairal Usón, R. (2005) Lexical representation based on a universal metalanguage. In *RAEL, Revista Española de Lingüística Aplicada. ISSN 1885-9089*, No. 4, pags. 125–73 http://dialnet.unirioja.es/servlet/extrev?codigo=6978

Hand, L. and McNeil, J. (2006) 'Being smart about Assessment SEDA', *Educational Developments*, 7 (4): 4–79–11.

Knight, P. and Yorke, M. (2003) *Assessment, Learning and Employability*. Maidenhead: SRHE/Open University Press.

Lamont, A. (2005) *Child of our time*. http://www.open2.net/childofourtime/2005/significance_music.html

McKeachie, W.J. (1994) *Teaching Tips*. Lexington, IL: D.C. Heath and Co.

Mortiboys, A. (2005) *Teaching with Emotional Intelligence*. London: Routledge.

Pickford, R. and Brown, S. (2006) *Assessing Skills and Practice*. London: Routledge.

Quinn, F.M. (2000) *Principles and Practices of Nurse Education* (4th edition), Cheltenham: Nelson Thornes.

Race, P. (2005) *Making Learning Happen*. London: Sage.

Race, P. (2006) *The Lecturer's Toolkit* (3rd edition). London: Routledge.

Sadler, D.R. (1989) 'Formative assessment and the design of instructional systems', *Instructional Science*, 18: 119–44.

Sadler, D.R. (1998) 'Formative assessment: revisiting the territory', *Assessment in Education: Principles, Policy and Practice*, 5: 77–84.

Sadler, D.R. (2003) 'How Criteria-based Grading Misses the Point'. Presentation to the Effective Teaching and Learning Conference, Griffith University, Australia.

Salmon, G. (2004) *E-moderating: The Key to Teaching and Learning On-line* (2nd edition). London: RoutledgeFalmer.

Salmon, G. (2007) Presentation at Teaching and Learning Conference, University of Leeds, 5 January.

Swain, H. (2006) 'Make Sure There is Room at the Inn', *Times Higher Education Supplement*, 22 December, p 34.

Yorke, M. (1999) *Leaving Early: Undergraduate Non-completion in Higher Education* London: Routledge.

Yorke, M. (2002) 'Academic Failure: A Retrospective View from Non-completing', in M. Peelo and T. Wareham (eds), *Failing Students in Higher Education*. Maidenhead: SRHE/Open University Press.

Yorke, M. and Longden, B. (2004) *Retention and Student Success in Higher Education*. Maidenhead: Open University Press.

Useful websites

Carnegie Academy for the Scholarship of Teaching and Learning
http://www.carnegiefoundation.org/programs/index.asp?key=21

HEFCE's TRAC methodology
http://www.hefce.ac.uk/learning/funding/trac/process.doc

SEDA
http://www.seda.ac.uk/professional_development.htm

Index